MW00529784

SPURGEON ON PERSEVERING THROUGH TRIALS

SPURGEON ON PERSEVERING THROUGH TRIALS

Spurgeon Speaks, Vol. 3

Compiled by

Jason K. Allen

MOODY PUBLISHERS

CHICAGO

© 2022 by
JASON K. ALLEN

All rights reserved. No part of this book may be reproduced in any form without permission in writing from the publisher, except in the case of brief quotations embodied in critical articles or reviews.

These sermons of Charles H. Spurgeon were originally published in the *Metropolitan Tabernacle Pulpit* and the *New Park Street Pulpit.* The compiler has sometimes shortened portions of these sermons and updated certain words and spelling for clarity and context. Scripture references have been updated to the New King James Version.

All Scripture quotations, unless otherwise indicated, are taken from the New King James Version. Copyright © 1982 by Thomas Nelson. Used by permission. All rights reserved.

Scripture quotations marked KJV are taken from the King James Version.

Edited by Allan Sholes
Interior design: Brandi Davis
Cover design: Gabriel Reyes-Ordeix
Cover illustration of Charles Spurgeon copyright © 2015 by denisk0/iStock (484302822). All rights reserved.

ISBN: 978-0-8024-2630-7

Originally delivered by fleets of horse-drawn wagons, the affordable paperbacks from D. L. Moody's publishing house resourced the church and served everyday people. Now, after more than 125 years of publishing and ministry, Moody Publishers' mission remains the same—even if our delivery systems have changed a bit. For more information on other books (and resources) created from a biblical perspective, go to www.moodypublishers.com or write to:

Moody Publishers
820 N. LaSalle Boulevard
Chicago, IL 60610

1 3 5 7 9 10 8 6 4 2

Printed in the United States of America

With profound appreciation, this book is dedicated to Bill and Connie Jenkins. Through God's kind providence, they are friends who have become like family. Under God's providence, the Spurgeon Library at Midwestern Seminary would not exist without their personal generosity.

Contents

Introduction

INFORMED READERS OF CHARLES SPURGEON know what distant admirers of the great man often do not—that the nineteenth century's greatest preacher struggled with depression throughout his adult life. It is true. Though Spurgeon soared to heights unknown in the pulpit, he often plummeted to depths unimaginable in his private life.

What drew the nineteenth century's most prominent preacher into the throes of depression? In addition to internal, organic factors that may have existed, we know of at least three significant, external factors: chronic illness, personal tragedy, and vocational trials.

Throughout his life, Spurgeon suffered from chronic illness. The limitations of nineteenth-century medicine exacerbated these ailments. Of particular note, for significant portions of his adult life Spurgeon suffered from gout and, most likely, Bright's disease. Few trials trouble the soul like unremitting physical pain. And that is exactly what Spurgeon endured throughout his life and ministry.

Spurgeon also experienced personal disasters. His beloved wife, Susannah, endured health challenges as well. Persistent gynecological problems culminated in major surgery in the late 1860s, leaving her in a near-invalid state. Thus, not only was Spurgeon burdened by his own health travails, but he was also anguished by seeing his beloved Susie similarly suffer and burdened by aiding her in times of need.

What is more, Spurgeon's early ministry was marred by the Surrey Gardens Music Hall catastrophe. With the attendance well surpassing the capacity limit of ten thousand guests, a prankster shouted "FIRE!" and sparked a stampede for the doors. In so doing, eight individuals were killed and dozens of others seriously injured. Spurgeon was so overwrought by the tragedy that he fell into a deep depression, so much so that he contemplated quitting the ministry and couldn't reenter the pulpit for weeks.

Lastly, Spurgeon endured seasons of vocational conflict (in his case, ministerial conflict). Spurgeon consistently defended the faith; he unwaveringly advocated for sound doctrine. Whether it was against Campbellism, Darwinism, Arminianism, or German Higher Criticism, Spurgeon always stood strong.

Never was this more clear than as seen through the prism of the Down-Grade Controversy, which resulted in Spurgeon being censured by the Baptist Union. Though history has long since vindicated the Prince of Preachers, the interpersonal fallout (and doctrinal compromise that prompted it) hurled Spurgeon, once again, into deep depression.

As you read this book, perhaps you find yourself in the throes of discouragement, if not outright depression. Or perhaps you know someone who is similarly struggling. I point you, through this book, not to Spurgeon, or even these edited sermons by him, but to the Savior they present.

And if you are downtrodden, may you one day reflect as did Spurgeon, "I find myself frequently depressed—perhaps more so than any other person here. And I find no better cure for that depression than to trust in the Lord with all my heart, and seek to realize afresh the power of the peace-speaking blood of Jesus, and His infinite love in dying upon the cross to put away my transgressions."[1]

So, dear friend, read this book carefully, reflect deeply on the spiritual nourishment within it, and, most of all, be strengthened in heart by the life-giving Word of God and the life-changing Savior, Jesus Christ, who is presented in it.

---

1. Charles Spurgeon, "The Secret of Happiness," Metropolitan Tabernacle, London, England, May 2, 1872.

TITLE:

The Trial of Your Faith

TEXT:

1 Peter 1:7

SUMMARY:

The faith given to God's elect is sweet and joy-filled. It brings light to the eyes and hope to the heart. However, the Christian should never expect trials to never venture his way. Christians must know that their faith will be tested, in a variety of ways, for God's purposes.

NOTABLE QUOTES:

"Wherever faith is found, it is the sure mark of eternal election, the sign of a blessed condition, the forecast of a heavenly destiny."

"Expect trial, also, because trial is the very element of faith."

"The trial of our faith is entirely in the hands of God."

1

The Trial of Your Faith

The trial of your faith.

1 PETER 1:7 KJV

IT IS A GREAT THING IF ANY MAN can truthfully speak to you, my brother, about "your faith," for wherever faith is found, it is the token of divine favor. True faith is of the operation of the Spirit of God. Its nature is purifying, elevating, heavenly. It is, of all things that can be cultivated in the human breast, one of the most precious. It is called "like precious faith," and it is styled "the faith of God's elect." Wherever faith is found, it is the sure mark of eternal election, the sign of a blessed condition, the forecast of a heavenly destiny. It is the eye of the renewed soul, the hand of the regenerated mind, the mouth of the new-born spirit. It is the evidence of spiritual life, the mainspring of holiness, the foundation of delight, the prophecy of glory, the dawn of endless knowledge.

If you have faith, you have infinitely more than he who has all the world and yet is destitute of faith. To him that believes it is said, "All things are yours." Faith is the assurance of sonship, the pledge of inheritance, the grasp of boundless possession, the perception of the invisible. Within your faith there lies glory, even as the oak sleeps within the acorn. If you have faith, you need not ask for much more, save that your faith may grow exceedingly and that all the promises which are made to it may be known and grasped by you. Time would fail me to tell of the powers, the privileges, the possessions, and the prospects of faith. He that has it is blessed, for he pleases God; he is justified before the throne of holiness, he has full access to the throne of grace, and he has the preparation for reigning with Christ forever.

So far everything is delightful. But then comes in this word, which somewhat startles, and, if we are cowardly, may also frighten—"The trial of your faith." See you the thorn which grows with this rose! You cannot gather the fragrant flower without its rough companion. You cannot possess the faith without experiencing the trial. These two things are put together—faith and trial; and it is of that trial of your faith that I am going to speak at this time. It may be, my brother, that words said at this good hour shall comfort you while you undergo the sorer trial of your faith. May the Holy Spirit, who nurtures faith, and preserves and perfects it under its trial, help our thoughts at this hour!

YOUR FAITH WILL BE TRIED

You may rest assured of that. A man may have faith and be for the present without trial, but no man ever had faith and was all his life without trial. That could not—must not—be; for faith, in the very nature of it, implies a degree of trial. I believe the promise of God. So far, my faith is tried in believing the promise, in waiting for the fulfillment of the promise, in holding on to an assurance of that promise while it is delayed, and in continuing to expect the promise and act upon it until it is fulfilled to me.

I do not see how faith can exist which is not tried by its own exercise. Take the very happiest and smoothest lives; there must be the trial of faith in taking the promise and pleading it before God in prayer and expecting its fulfillment. God never gave us faith to play with. It is a sword, but it was not made for presentation. It is meant to cut and wound and slay; and he that has it may expect, between here and heaven, that he shall know what battle means. Faith is a sound seagoing vessel and was not meant to lie in dock and perish of dry rot.

The very gift of faith is a hint to you that you will want it, that at certain points and places you will especially require it, and that at all points you will really need it. You cannot live without faith, for again and again we are told "the just shall live by faith." Believing is our living, and we, therefore, need it always. And if God give you great faith, you must expect great trials, for in proportion as your faith shall grow, you will have to do more and endure more. Little boats may keep close to shore, but if God make you a great vessel, He means that ı shouldest know what great billows are. That God, who has made nothing in vain, especially makes nothing in the spiritual kingdom in vain; and if He makes faith, it is with the design that it should be used to the utmost and exercised to the full.

Expect trial, also, because trial is the very element of faith. Faith is a diamond which bores its way through the rock. Faith without trial is like a diamond uncut, the brilliance of which has never been seen. Untried faith is such little faith that some have thought it no faith at all. What a fish would be without water, or a bird without air, that would be faith without trial. If you have faith, you may surely expect that your faith will be tested: the great Keeper of the treasures admits no coin to His coffers without testing. It is so in the nature of faith, and so in the order of its living: it thrives not, save in such weather as might seem to threaten its death.

Indeed, it is the honor of faith to be tried. Shall any man say, "I have faith, but I have never had to believe under difficulties"? Who knows whether you have any faith? Shall a man say, "I have great faith in God, but I have never had to use it in anything more than the ordinary affairs of life, where I could probably have done without it as well as with it"? Is this to the honor and praise of your faith? Do you think that such a faith as this will bring any great glory to God, or bring to you any great reward? If so, you are mightily mistaken.

Had Abraham stopped in Ur of the Chaldees with his friends, and rested there, and enjoyed himself, where had been his faith? He had God's command to quit his country to go to a land he had never seen, to sojourn there with God as a stranger, dwelling in tents; and in his obedience to that call his faith began to be illustrious. Where had been the glory of his faith if it had not been called to brave and self-denying deeds? Would he ever have risen to that supreme height, to be "the father of the faithful," if he had not grown old, and his body dead, and yet he had believed that God would give him seed of his aged wife Sarah according to the promise? It was blessed faith that made him feel that nothing was impossible to God.

If Isaac had been born to him in the days of his strength, where had been his faith? And when it came to that more severe test to sacrifice Isaac, then was his faith confessed, commended, and crowned. Then the Lord said, "Now I know," as if, even to God, the best evidence of Abraham's faith had then been displayed when he staggered not at the promise through unbelief, reckoning that God could restore Isaac from the dead if need be, but that it was his to obey the supreme command and trust all consequences with God, who could not lie. Herein his faith won great renown, and he became "the father of the faithful," because he was the most tried of believers and yet surpassed them all in childlike belief in his God.

We remember also two reasons for the trial of faith. The trial of your faith is sent to prove its sincerity. If it will not stand trial, what is the good of it? That gold which dissolves in the furnace is not the gold which shall be current with the merchant; and that faith of yours, which is no sooner tried than straightway it evaporates, are you not well rid of it? Of what use would it be to you in the hour of death and in the day of judgment? No, you cannot be sure that your faith is true faith till it is tried faith.

It must also be tested to prove its strength. We sometimes fancy that we have strong faith when, indeed, our faith is very weak; and how are we to know whether it be weak or strong till it be tried? A man that should lie in bed week after week, and perhaps get the idle whim into his head that he was very strong, would be pretty certain to be mistaken. It is only when he sets about work requiring muscular strength that he will discover how strong or how weak he is. God would not have us form a wrong estimate of ourselves. He loves not that we should say that we are rich and increased in goods and have need of nothing when we are the reverse; and therefore He sends to us the trial of our faith that we may understand how strong or how weak it is.

Besides that, dear friends, the trial of our faith is necessary to remove its dross. There are many accretions of sordid matter about our purest graces. We are apt ourselves to add to the bulk of our graces without adding to the real value of them. We mistake quantity for quality, and a great deal of what we think we have of Christian experience, knowledge, zeal, and patience is only the supposition that we have these graces and not their real possession. So the fire grows fiercer, and the mass grows smaller than it was before. Is there any loss therein? I think not. The gold loses nothing by the removal of its dross, and our faith loses nothing by the dissipation of its apparent force. Faith may apparently lose, but it actually gains. It may seem to be diminished, but it is not truly diminished. All is there that was worth having. You can now tell how much was solid and how much was sham, for had that which has failed you been real faith, it would not have been consumed by any trial through which it has passed. You have lost the froth from the top of the cup, but all that was really worth having is still there.

Understand, then, that for many necessary purposes there is a need for trial. Peter says here, "If need be" that there should be a trial of your faith. You will get that trial, because God, in His wisdom, will give faith what faith needs. Do not be anxious to enter into trial. Do not fret if temptation does not come just now. You will have it soon enough. We need not be uneasy if for a while we are at ease, for there are months enough left to the year to give winter its full measure of frosts and storms.

YOUR FAITH WILL BE TRIED

Trial of our faith does not come to all persons in the same way. There are some whose faith is tried each day in their communion with God. They pray this prayer: "Search me, O God, and know my heart: try me, and know my anxieties: and see if there is any wicked way in me; and lead me in the way everlasting." That prayer is heard constantly; the visitations of the Lord are granted to them, and as the Lord comes, He tries them; for, believe me, there is no surer trial of our souls than the drawing near of God to our souls. If you walk away from God, you may retain in your heart much falsehood and fancy that you are full of spiritual gifts and graces, but if you draw near to God, you will not be able to retain a false opinion of yourself.

Remember what the Lord is. Our God is a consuming fire. When His people live in Him, the very presence of God consumes in them their love of sin and all their pretentious graces and fictitious attainments, so that the false disappears and only the true survives. The presence of perfect holiness kills empty boasting and hollow pretense. You need not ask for any of those various forms of trial which God sends in the order of providence: you may rest quite satisfied with His presence. It is the Lord Himself that will be as a refiner's fire and like fullers' soap. Who may abide the day of His coming? Who that loves holiness would wish to escape it?

Ay, let the devouring flame go through me, and through me yet again, till this earthly grossness shall begin to disappear. As Moses soon put his shoes off from his feet when he beheld God at the burning bush, so shall we put off the superfluities of our supposed spiritual experience and come to the real, naked foot of truth, if we are permitted to stand before God in accepted sincerity. Thus you see there is a constant trial of our faith, even in that which is its greatest joy and glory, namely its power to make us see the Lord.

But the Lord uses other methods with His servants. I believe that He frequently tries us by the blessings He sends us. When a man is permitted to grow rich, what a trial of faith is hidden away in that condition! It is one of the severest of providential tests! Where I have known one man fail through poverty, I have known fifty men fail through riches. When our friends have a long stretch of prosperity, they should invite their brethren to offer special prayer for them, that they may be preserved. When we do not cling to wealth, it will not harm us; but there is a deal of birdlime in money.

You that have no riches may yet find a test in your daily

mercies: your domestic comfort, that loving wife, those dear children—all these may tempt you to walk by sight instead of by faith. Ay, and continued health, the absence of all depression of spirit, and the long abiding of friends and relatives may all make you self-contented and keep you away from your God. It is a great trial of faith to have much for sight to rest upon. To be in the dark—altogether in the dark—is a grand thing for faith, for then you are sure that what you see is not seen of the flesh but is in very deed a vision of spiritual faith. To be under a cloud is a trial, truly, but not one-half so much a trial as it is to have continually the light of this world. We are so apt to mistake the light of carnal comfort for the light of God, that it is well to see how we fare without it.

One form of this trial is praise. You know how Solomon puts it: "As the fining pot for silver, and the furnace for gold; so is a man to his praise" (KJV). A Christian minister may go on preaching very earnestly, and God will help him though everybody opposes him. But when the world comes and pats him on the back, and pride whispers, "You are a fine fellow; you are a great man!" then comes the test of the man. How few there are that can endure the warm atmosphere of congratulation! It is dangerously relaxing to the spirit. Yea, nobody can keep himself right under it, unless the almighty grace of God shall sustain his faith. When the soft winds blow, they bring with them the temptation, "Now preach the doctrines that tickle men's ears!" And unless you say, "Get behind me, Satan! . . . you are not mindful of the things of God," such a trial of faith may be too much for you.

Because of your natural attainments and the amiability of your temper, you may become a great favorite with ungodly people, and that is an intense trial to the faith of a child of God. The friendship of the world is as much enmity with God as it used to be in apostolic times. It is a bad sign when a courtier is in great favor with the king's enemies. Stand up and stand out as the servant of God, and in whatever sphere you move, make it your one and only business to serve my God, whether you offend or please. Happy shall you be if you survive the trial of your faith which this will involve!

Another trial of faith is exceedingly common and perilous nowadays: heretical doctrine and false teaching. Some are carried away with this wind of doctrine, and others carried away with the other, and blessed is he who is not offended in Christ; for, naturally, the cross of Christ is offensive to the minds of men. There are temptations that rise out of the gospel itself, yea, out of its very depth and breadth. There is a trial of faith in reading the Scriptures. You come across a doctrine you cannot understand, and because you cannot understand it you are tempted not to receive it. Or, when a truth which you have received appears to be hard and speaks to you in an unlovely fashion so that your natural feelings are aroused against it, this is a trial of your faith. Remember how our Lord Jesus lost quite a company of disciples on a certain occasion. He had taught a doctrine about eating His flesh and drinking His blood, and from that hour many went back, and walked no more with Him, till the Savior had to say, even to the twelve, "Do you also want to go away?"

Truth is not always welcome to our ignorance, or to our prejudice, and herein is a trial of faith. Will we believe ourselves or our God? Do we want to believe God's truth, or do we wish to have the Lord's message flavored to our taste? Do we expect the preacher to play our chosen tunes and speak our opinions? Beloved, it does us good to be well rasped sometimes, to have a word come to us, not as a sweet wine but as a purging medicine. If we run in the same line with God's truth, we are true, but when we run counter to the truth of God, we are ourselves untrue. It is not the Book that is to be altered; our hearts want altering.

But the trial of our faith usually comes in the form of affliction. Our jealous Lover uses tests that it may be seen whether He has our heart. The trial of your faith comes thus: You say, "Lord Jesus, I love you. You are my best beloved." "Well," says the heavenly Lover, "if it be so, then the child that nestles in your bosom will sicken and die. What will you say then?" If you be indeed true in what you have stated concerning your supreme love to Jesus, you will give up your darling at His call. The Lord is very jealous of our love. I do not mean that He is so towards all of you: I speak of His own people. The more He loves us, the more He tests us. Whatever it may be with us poor creatures, it is always so with Jesus, that His love goes with His jealousy, and His jealousy with His love.

My Lord sometimes comes to me in this fashion. He says, "I have made you to trust Me these many years. I have supplied the wants of your work by generous friends. I am about to remove a generous helper." I go to the grave of my friend, and the suggestion dogs me, "Who is to provide for the orphanage and the college, after other dear friends are buried? Can you trust God then?" Blessed be the name of the Lord, this fiery trial has never even left the smell of fire upon me; I know whom I have believed. If you once get to walk the walk of faith, the Lord will often try you in this way, to see whether you come up to your own confession—whether you really trust in the Lord.

If every earthly prop were knocked away, could you stand by the lone power of your foundation? God may not send you this or that trial, but He will send you a sufficient amount of trial to let you see whether your faith is truth or talk, whether you have truly entered the spiritual world or have only dreamed of doing so. Believe me, there is a great difference between a diamond and a paste gem, and the Lord would not have mistaken at the last.

YOUR FAITH WILL BE TRIED INDIVIDUALLY

It is not quite so pleasant to study alone the trial of your faith. It is stern work when it comes to be your trial, and the trial of your faith. You have not gone much into that particular department, perhaps. Well, I say again, do not wish to do so. Do not ask for trials. Children must not ask to be whipped, nor saints pray to be tested. There is a little book which you will have to eat, and it will be bitter in your mouth but sweet in your bowels: the trial of your faith. The Lord Jesus Christ has been glorified by the trial of His people's faith. He has to be glorified by the trial of your faith.

You are very obscure, perhaps, dear brother. You have but few talents, my dear sister. But, nevertheless, there is a particular shape and form of trial that will have to be exercised upon you rather than upon anyone else. If you know it, do not complain of it; because when you have your own trial, and the trial of your own faith, you are only treated like the rest of the family. What son is there whom the father disciplines not? You are only treated like the Head of the family. You are only treated in the way which the great Father of the family knows is necessary for us all.

God had one Son without sin, but He never had a son without trial, and He never will have until He has taken us all home out of this world. Why should we expect that God should deal better with us than He does with the rest of His chosen? Indeed, it would not be better, after all, because these trials are the means of working out our lasting good. But if it were not so, who am I, and who are you, that God should pamper us? Would we have Him put us in a glass case and shield us from the trials which are common to all the chosen seed? I ask no such portion. Let me fare as the saints fare. The trial of our faith will be all our own, and yet it will be in fellowship with all the family of grace.

YOUR FAITH WILL BE TRIED SEARCHINGLY

It will be no child's play to come under the divine tests. Our faith is not merely jingled on the counter like the shilling which the tradesman suspects, but it is tried with fire; for so it is written, "I have tested you in the furnace of affliction." The blows of the flail of tribulation are not given in sport, but in awful earnest, as some of us know who have been chastened sore, almost unto death. The Lord tries the very life of our faith;

not its beauty and its strength alone, but its very existence. The iron enters into the soul; the sharp medicine searches the inmost parts of the belly; the man's real self is made to endure the trial. It is easy to talk of being tried, but it is by no means so simple a matter to endure the ordeal.

YOUR FAITH WILL BE TRIED
FOR A USEFUL PURPOSE

The trial of your faith will increase, develop, deepen, and strengthen it. "Oh," you have said, "I wish I had more faith." Your prayer will be heard through you having more trial. Often in our prayers we have sought for a stronger faith to look within the veil. The way to stronger faith usually lies along the rough pathway of sorrow. Only as faith is contested will faith be confirmed.

I do not know whether my experience is that of all God's people, but the good that I have received from my sorrows, pains, and griefs is altogether incalculable. What do I not owe to the hammer and the anvil, the fire and the file? What do I not owe to the crucible and the furnace, the bellows that have blown up the coals, and the hand which has thrust me into the heat? Affliction is the best book in a minister's library. We may wisely rejoice in tribulation because it works patience, and patience experience, and experience hope; and by that way we are exceedingly enriched and our faith grows strong.

The trial of our faith is useful, not only because it strengthens it but because it leads to a discovery of our faith to ourselves.

When affliction comes into the soul and makes a disturbance and breaks our peace, up rise our graces. Faith comes out of its hiding, and love leaps from its secret place. Often in the days of our prosperity we fail to find our faith; but when our adversity comes, the winter of our trial bares the boughs, and we see our faith at once. We are sure that we believe now, for we feel the effect of faith upon our character. It is a great mercy, then, to have your faith tried, that you may be sure beyond all manner of question that you are a true believer.

This trial of our faith does good to our fellow Christians. They see how we are supported, and they learn to bear their troubles bravely. I do not know anything that is better for making us brave than to see others believe in Christ and bear up manfully. To see that blind saint so happy makes us ashamed to be sad. To see content in an inmate of the workhouse compels us to be thankful. Sufferers are our tutors; they educate us for the skies. When men of God can suffer, when they can bear poverty, bereavement, or sickness and still rejoice in God, we learn the way to live the higher and more Christly life.

When Patrick Hamilton had been burned in Scotland, one said to his persecutors, "If you are going to burn anymore, you had better do it in a cellar, for the smoke of Hamilton's burning has opened the eyes of hundreds." It was always so. Suffering saints are living seed. Oh, that God might help us to such faith, that when we come to suffer in life, or to expire in death, we may so glorify God that others may believe in Him! May we preach sermons by our faith which shall be better than sermons in words.

SOME ARE TRIED SPECIALLY

Some endure many more tests than others, and that is because God has a great favor to them. Many men God does not love well enough to whip them. They are the devil's children, and the heavenly Father does not trouble them. They are none of His, and so He lets them have a happy life, and perhaps an easy death. But they are to be pitied and not envied. Woe unto you that laugh now, for you shall weep! Woe unto you who have your portion in this life, for it shall go ill with you in the world to come! God's children are often much chastened because they are much loved. Men take most trouble with that which is most precious. A common pebble will be let alone, but a diamond must be fretted on the wheel till its brilliance is displayed.

Some persons are also much tried in their faith because they are very fit for it. God has fitted the back for a heavy burden, and the burden will be sent. He has constituted them on purpose that they should be helpful in filling up "that which is behind of the afflictions of Christ in my flesh for his body's sake, which is the church." Men build strong columns because they are meant to carry great weights. So God makes great Christians that they should bear great afflictions for His glory.

He does this also because He would have some men do Him a special service. What an honor it is to do the Lord a special service! If any of you are brave in bearing affliction, you shall have the honor of enduring more affliction. Does not every soldier court the opportunity of service? He that looks over his soldiers says of a certain one, "I shall not send him; he is feeble and faint-hearted; yonder veteran is the man for me." Do not think that you would be honored by being allowed to ride to heaven on a feather bed. True honor lies in being permitted to bear and suffer side by side with Him of the bloody sweat and of the five open wounds. This is the guerdon of the saints, that they should on earth be decorated with "many a sorrow, many a tear." They shall walk with their Lord in white, for they are worthy.

Yes, dear friends, the Lord often sends us greater trials than others because He means to qualify us for greater enjoyments. If you want to make a pool capable of holding more water, you dig it out, do you not? And many a man has been dug and enlarged by affliction. The enlargements of trial enable us to hold more grace and more glory. The more a gracious man suffers, the more he becomes capable of entering into fellowship with Christ in His sufferings, and so into fellowship with Christ in His glory by-and-by.

Come, let us be comforted as to the trial of our faith. There is no hurt in it. It is all for good. The trial of our faith is entirely in the hands of God. Nobody can try us without God's permission. He will try us just as much as we ought to be tried, and no more. While He tries us with one hand, He will sustain us with the other. If He gives us bitters, He will give us sweets in full proportion.

Some of us have cried, "Take me back to my sickness again. Take me back to slander and rebuke again." Our worst days are often our best days, and in the dark we see stars that we never saw in the light. So we will not care a pin what it is that may befall us here, so long as God is with us and our faith in Him is genuine. Christian people, I am not going to condole with you, but I congratulate you upon your troubles, for the cross of Christ is precious.

But you that do not love my Lord and Master, if you roll in riches, if your eyes stand out with fatness, I mourn over you. Bullocks fattened for the slaughter, your joys are but the prelude to your woes. Oh, that God would have mercy upon you, and that you would have mercy upon yourselves and flee at once to Jesus and put your trust in Him! Faith in the work, offices, and person of the Lord Jesus is the way of salvation. May He help you to run in it at this hour, for His name's sake! Amen.

TITLE:
All Joy in All Trials

TEXT:
James 1:2–4

SUMMARY:
The reality of the Christian life is that each Christian will undergo temptations and trials. Not at every moment are we individually experiencing such trials, but at all points some Christians are. Therefore, when we are tried, we must remember that it is our faith that is being tried. It is our enemy's main focus of attack. However, the Christian does not undergo trials needlessly; it proves our faith, causes us to cling to God, and brings us back to the throne of grace so that we may be found complete—lacking nothing.

NOTABLE QUOTES:
"Our chief end is to glorify God, and if our trials enable us more fully to answer the end of our being, it is well that they should happen unto us."

"Two little words are good for every Christian to learn and to practice—pray and stay."

"We are not to try ourselves, nor to desire other men's trials; it will be well if we endure those the Lord appoints for us, for they will be wisely chosen."

2

All Joy
in All Trials

My brethren, count it all joy when you fall into various trials, knowing that the testing of your faith produces patience. But let patience have its perfect work, that you may be perfect and complete, lacking nothing.

JAMES 1:2–4

JAMES CALLS THE CONVERTED among the twelve tribes his brethren. Christianity has a great uniting power: it both discovers and creates relationships among people. It reminds us of the ties of nature and binds us with the bonds of grace. Every one born of the Spirit of God is brother to every other born of the same Spirit. Well may we be called brethren, for we are redeemed by one blood; we are partakers of the same life; we feed upon the same heavenly food; we are united to the same living head; we seek the same ends; we love the same Father. We are heirs of the same promises; and we shall dwell forever together in the same heaven. Let brotherly love continue; let us love one another with a pure heart fervently and manifest that love, not in word only but in deed and in truth. Whatever brotherhood may be a sham, let the brotherhood of believers be the most real thing beneath the stars.

Beginning with this word, "brethren," James shows a true brotherly sympathy with believers in their trials, and this is a main part of Christian fellowship. If we are not tempted ourselves at this moment, others are. Let us remember them in our prayers, for in due time our turn will come, and we shall be put into the crucible. As we would desire to receive sympathy and help in our hour of need, let us render it freely to those who are now enduring trial. Let us remember those that are in bonds as bound with them, and those that suffer affliction as being ourselves also in the body. Remembering the trials of his brethren, James tries to cheer them, and therefore he says, "My brethren, count it all joy when you fall into various trials." It is a part of our high calling to rise ourselves into confidence; and it is also our duty to see that none of our brethren despond, much less despair.

The whole tendency of our holy faith is to elevate and to encourage. Grace breeds no sorrow, except the healthier sorrow which comes with saving repentance and leads to the joy of pardon. It comes not to make men miserable but to wipe all tears from their eyes. Our dream is not of devils descending a dreary staircase to hell but of angels ascending and descending upon a ladder, the top of which leads to the shining throne of God.

The message of the gospel is one of joy and gladness and, were it universally understood and received, this world would be no longer a wilderness, but it would rejoice and blossom as the rose. Let grace reign in all hearts, and this earth will become a temple filled with perpetual song. Even the trials of life will become causes of the highest joy, so beautifully described by James as "all joy," as if every possible delight were crowded into it. Blessed be God, it is our work not to upbraid but to cheer all the brotherhood. We are able to speak with the afflicted and bid them be patient under the chastening hand of God, yea, to count it all joy when they fall into various trials because those trials will work out for them such signal, such lasting good. They may be well content to sow in tears since they are sure to reap in joy.

Without further preface we will come at once to the text and observe that in speaking about affliction, the apostle notes first the essential point, which is assailed by temptation, namely, your faith. Your faith is the target that all the arrows are shot at; the furnace is kindled for the trial of your faith. Notice, secondly, the invaluable blessing which is thus gained, namely, the proving of your faith, discovering whether it be the right faith or no. This proof of our faith is a blessing of which I cannot speak too highly. Then, thirdly, we may not overlook the priceless virtue which is produced by this process of testing, namely, patience; for the proving of your faith produces patience, and this is the soul's surest enrichment. Lastly, in connection with that patience we shall note the spiritual completeness which is thus promoted: "that you may be perfect and complete, lacking nothing."

THE ESSENTIAL POINT WHICH IS ASSAILED

It is your faith which is tried. It is supposed that you have that faith. It is this faith of yours which is peculiarly obnoxious to Satan and to the world. If you had no faith, they would not be your enemies. But faith is the mark of the chosen of God, and therefore His foes become the foes of all the faithful. God Himself has put enmity between the serpent and the woman, between the serpent's seed and the woman's seed, and that enmity must show itself. The serpent bites at the heel of the true seed, hence mockings, persecutions, temptations, and trials are sure to beset the pathway of faith. The hand of faith is against all evil, and all evil is against faith. Faith is that blessed grace which is most pleasing to God, and hence it is most displeasing to the devil. By faith God is greatly glorified, and hence by faith Satan is greatly annoyed. He rages at faith because he sees therein his own defeat and the victory of grace.

Because the trial of your faith brings honor to the Lord, the Lord Himself is sure to try it, that out of its trial praise may come to His grace by which faith is sustained. Our chief end is to glorify God, and if our trials enable us more fully to answer the end of our being, it is well that they should happen unto us.

It is by our faith that we are saved, justified, and brought near to God, and therefore it is no marvel that it is attacked. It is by believing in Christ that we are delivered from the reigning power of sin and receive power to become the sons of God. Faith is as vital to salvation as the heart is vital to the body; hence the javelins of the enemy are mainly aimed at this essential grace. Faith is the standard bearer, and the object of the enemy is to strike him down that the battle may be gained. If the foundations be removed, what can the righteous do? All the powers of darkness which are opposed to right and truth are sure to fight against our faith, and manifold temptations will march in their legions against our confidence in God.

It is by our faith that we live; we began to live by it, and we continue to live by it, for "the just shall live by faith." Once let faith go and our life is gone; and hence it is that the powers which war against us make their main assault upon this royal castle, this key of the whole position. Faith is your jewel, your joy, your glory, and the thieves who haunt the pilgrim way are all in league to tear it from you. Hold fast, therefore, this your choice treasure.

It is by faith, too, that Christians perform exploits. If men of old wrought daring and heroic deeds, it was by faith. Rob a Christian of his faith, and he will be like Samson when his locks were cut away. Marvel not if the full force of the current shall beat upon your faith, for it is the foundation of your spiritual house. Oh that your faith may abide steadfast and unmovable in all present trials, that so it may be found true in the hour of death and in the day of judgment. Woe unto that man whose faith fails him in this land of peace, for what will he do in the swellings of Jordan?

Now think of how faith is tried. According to the text we are said to fall into "various trials"—that is to say, we may expect very many and very different troubles. In any case, these trials will be most real. The twelve tribes to whom this epistle was written were a specially tried people, for in the first place they were, as Jews, greatly persecuted by all other nations, and when they became Christians they were cruelly persecuted by their own people. A Gentile convert was somewhat less in peril than a Jewish Christian, for the latter was crushed between the upper and the nether millstones of paganism and Judaism. The Israelitish Christian was usually so persecuted by his own kith and kin that he had to flee from them, and whither could he go, for all other people abhorred the Jews?

We are not in such a plight, but God's people even to this day will find that trial is no sham word. The rod in God's house is no toy to play with. The furnace, believe me, is no mere place of extra warmth. Our temptations are no inventions of nervousness nor hobgoblins of dreamy fear. You have heard of the patience of Job—his was real patience, for his afflictions were real.

Ay, and note too, that the trials of Christians are such as would in themselves lead us into sin. The natural tendency of trouble is not to sanctify, but to induce sin. A man is very apt to become unbelieving under affliction: that is a sin. He is apt to murmur against God under it: that is a sin. He is apt to put forth his hand to some ill way of escaping from his difficulty, and that would be a sin. Hence we are taught to pray, "Lead us not into temptation," because trial has in itself a measure of temptation, and if it were not neutralized by abundant grace, it would bear us towards sin.

I suppose that every test must have in it a measure of temptation. The Lord cannot be tempted of evil, neither tempt He any man; but this is to be understood of His end and design. He entices no man to do evil, but He tries the sincerity and faithfulness of men by placing them where sin comes in their way and does its best or its worst to ensnare them, His design being that the uprightness of His servants may thus be proved, both to themselves and others. We are not taken out of this world of temptation, but we are kept in it for our good. Do I not speak to many here who at times feel strong impulses towards evil, especially in the darksome hour when the spirit of evil walks abroad? Have you not been made to tremble for yourselves in seasons of fierce trial? Is there any virtue that has not been weather-beaten? Is there any love that has not at times been so tried that it threatened to curdle into hate? Did ever a flower of grace blossom in this wretched clime without being tried with frost or blight? Thus, not only trials but black temptations assail the Christian's faith.

As to what shape they take, we may say this much: the trial or temptation of each man is distinct from that of every other. When God did tempt Abraham he was bidden to take his son, his only son, and offer him upon a mountain for a sacrifice. Nobody here was ever tried in that way: nobody ever will be. We may have the trial of losing our child, but certainly not the trial of having a command to offer him in sacrifice.

In the case of the young man in the Gospels, our Lord Jesus tried him with, "If you want to be perfect, go, sell what you have and give to the poor, and you will have treasure in heaven." Some have dreamed that it must therefore be the duty of everybody to part with their possessions, but this is idle. It would not be the duty of any man to offer up his only son; and it is not the duty of every man to part with all his goods.

We are not to try ourselves, nor to desire other men's trials; it will be well if we endure those the Lord appoints for us, for they will be wisely chosen. That which would most severely test me would perhaps be no trial to you; and that which tries you might be no temptation to me. This is one reason why we often judge one another so severely, because feeling ourselves to be strong in that particular point, we argue that the fallen one must have been strong in that point too, and therefore must have willfully determined to do wrong. This may be a cruel supposition. We hastily conclude that the temptation must have been as feeble in his case as it would have been in our own. This is a great mistake, for a temptation which to you or to me would be no temptation at all, may be to another individual a most fierce and terrible blast from the adversary, before which he falls mournfully but not with malice aforethought.

And, dear friends, sometimes these divers [KJV] trials derive great force from their seemingly surrounding us and cutting off escape. James says, "You fall into various trials," like men who fall into a pit and do not know how to get out. The tempted see not which way to turn; they appear to be hemmed in, as a bird that is taken in the fowler's snare. This makes calamity of our manifold temptations, that they hedge up our way, and unless faith finds the clue we wander in a thorny maze.

At times temptation comes suddenly upon us, and so we fall into it. When we were at rest, suddenly the evil came, like a lion leaping from the thicket. When Job's children were eating and drinking in their elder brother's house, then suddenly a wind came from the wilderness, and the patriarch was bereaved. The cattle were plowing, the sheep were grazing, the camels were at their service, and in a moment, by fire from heaven and by robber bands, the whole of these possessions vanished. One messenger had not told his story before another followed at his heels. Job had no breathing time; the blows fell thick and fast. The trial of our faith is most severe when divers trials happen to us when we look not for them. Is it not strange in the light of those things that James should say, "Count it all joy when you fall into various trials"?

Those were the days of tumults, imprisonment, crucifixion, sword, and fire. Then the amphitheater devoured Christians by thousands. The general cry was "The Christians to the lions!" Do you wonder if sometimes the bravest were made to say, "Is our faith really true? This faith which is abhorred of all mankind, can it be divine? Has it come from God? Why, then, does He not interpose and deliver His people? Shall we apostatize? Shall we deny Christ and live, or shall we go on with our confession through innumerable torments even to a bloody death? Will fidelity answer after all? Is there a crown of glory? Is there an eternity of bliss? Is there in very deed a resurrection of the dead?" These questions came into men's minds then and were fairly laced. The faith of martyrs was not taken up secondhand or borrowed from their parents; they believed for themselves in downright earnest. Men and women in those days believed in such a way that they never flinched nor started aside from fear of death; indeed, they pressed forward to confess their faith in Jesus in such crowds that at last the heathen cried, "There must be something in it: it must be a religion of God, or how could these men so gladly bear their troubles?" This was the faith of God's elect, the work of the Holy Ghost.

THE BLESSING GAINED
BY THE TRIAL OF OUR FAITH

The blessing gained is this: that our faith is tried and proved. The effectual proof is by trials of God's sending. The way of trying whether you are a good soldier is to go down to the battle. The way to try whether a ship is well built is to send her to sea: a storm will be the best test of her staunchness. We need trials as a test as much as we need divine truth as our food.

Admire the ancient types placed in the ark of the covenant of old. Two things were laid close together: the pot of manna and the rod [Heb. 9:4]. See how heavenly food and heavenly rule go together, how our sustenance and our chastening are equally provided for! A Christian cannot live without the manna nor without the rod. The two must go together. I mean that it is as great a mercy to have your salvation proved to you under trial as it is to have it sustained in you by the consolations of the Spirit of God. Sanctified tribulations work the proof of our faith, and this is more precious than that of gold.

Now, when we are able to bear it without starting aside, the trial proves our sincerity. Coming out of a trouble the Christian says to himself, "Yes, I held fast my integrity and did not let it go. Blessed be God, I was not afraid of threatening; I was not crushed by losses; I was kept true to God under pressure. Now I am sure that my religion is not a mere profession but a real consecration to God. It has endured the fire, being kept by the power of God."

Next, it proves the truthfulness of our doctrinal belief. If you have been sick and found a comfort in those doctrines, then you are assured of their truth. If you have been on the borders of the grave, and the gospel has given you joy and gladness, then you know how true it is. Experimental knowledge is the best and surest. If you have seen others pass through death itself triumphantly, you have said, "This is proof to me. I have seen for myself." Is not this assurance cheaply purchased at any price? May we not count it all joy when the Lord puts us in the way of getting it? It seems to me that doubt is worse than trial. I had sooner suffer any affliction than be left to question the gospel or my own interest in it. Certainly it is a jewel worth purchasing even with our heart's blood.

Next, your own faith in God is proved when you can cling to Him under temptation. Not only your sincerity but the divinity of your faith is proved, for how can you depend on a faith that is never tried? But if in the darkest hour you have still said, "I cast my burden upon the Lord, and He will sustain me," and you find He does sustain you, then is your faith that of God's elect. If in temptation you cry to God in prayer that you may keep your garment unspotted, and He helps you to do so, then also are you sure that yours is the faith which the Spirit begets in the soul.

I find it specially sweet to learn the great strength of the Lord in my own weakness. We find out under trial where we are most weak, and just then in answer to prayer strength is given answerable to the need. The Lord suits the help to the hindrance and puts the plaster on the wound. In the very hour when it is needed, the needed grace is given. Does not this tend to breed assurance of faith?

It is a splendid thing to be able to prove even to Satan the purity of your motives. That was the great gain of Job. There was no question about his outward conduct, but the question was about his motive. Well, he is tried, and everything is taken away, and when he cries, "Though He slay me, yet will I trust in Him," when he blesses the taking as well as the giving God, then the devil himself could not have the impudence to accuse him again. As to Job's own conscience, it would be quite settled and confirmed as to his pure love to God. My brethren, I reckon that the endurance of every imaginable suffering and trial would be a small price to pay for a settled assurance. Never mind the waves if they wash you upon this rock. Therefore, when you are tempted, "count it all joy" that you are tried, because you will thus receive a proof of your love, a proof of your faith, a proof of your being the true-born children of God.

James says, "Count it." A man requires to be trained to be a good accountant; it is an art which needs to be learned. What muddles some of us would make if we had to settle accounts and manage disbursements and incomings without the aid of a clerk! How we should get entangled with balances and deficits! We could much easier spend money than count it. But when a man once knows the science of bookkeeping, he readily arrives at the true position of affairs. He has learned to count, and no error escapes his eye.

James gives us a ready reckoner and teaches us in our troubles how to count. He sets before us a different kind of measure from that which carnal reason would use: the shekel of the sanctuary was very different from the shekel in common commerce, and so is the counting of faith far other than that of human judgment. He bids us take our pen and sit down quickly and write at his correct dictation. You were going to write down, "Manifold temptations." That would be so much on the wrong side, but thereof he bids you set down the proving of your faith, and this one asset transforms the transaction into a substantial gain. Trials are like a fire; they burn up nothing in us but the dross, and they make the gold all the purer. Instead of being sorry about it, count it all joy when you fall into divers trials, for this bestows upon you a proof of your faith.

THE PRICELESS VIRTUE PRODUCED BY TRIAL

The proof of your "faith works patience." Patience! We all have a large stock of it—until we need it, and then we have none. The man who truly possesses patience is the man that has been tried. What kind of patience does he get by the grace of God? First, he obtains a patience that accepts the trial as from God without a murmur. Calm resignation does not come all at once; often long years of physical pain, or mental depression, or disappointment in business, or multiplied bereavements are needed to bring the soul into full submission to the will of the Lord. By degrees we learn to end our quarrel with God, and to desire that God's will may be our will. Oh, brother, if your troubles work you to that, you are a gainer, and you may count them all joy.

The next kind of patience is when experience enables a man to bear ill-treatment, slander, and injury without resentment. He feels it keenly, but he bears it meekly. Like his Master, he opens not his mouth to reply and refuses to return railing for railing. Contrariwise he gives blessing in return for cursing; like the sandalwood tree which perfumes the axe which cuts it. Ah, friend, if the grace of God by trial shall work in you the quiet patience which never grows angry and never ceases to love, you may have lost a trifle of comfort, but you have gained a solid weight of character.

The patience which God works in us by tribulation also takes another form, namely, that of acting without undue haste. Before wisdom has balanced our zeal, we are eager to serve God all in a hurry, as if everything must be done within the hour or nothing would ever be accomplished. We set about holy service with somewhat more of preparedness of heart after we have been drilled in the school of trial. We go steadily and resolutely about work for Jesus, knowing what poor creatures we are, and what a glorious Master we serve. The Lord our God is in no hurry because He is strong and wise. In proportion as we grow like the Lord Jesus we shall cast aside disturbance of mind and fury of spirit. His was a grand lifework, but He never seemed to be confused, excited, worried, or hurried. He did not strive nor cry, nor cause His voice to be heard in the streets. He knew His hour was not yet come, and there were so many days in which He could work, and therefore He went steadily on till He had finished the work which His Father had given Him to do. That kind of patience is a jewel more to be desired than the gem which glitters on the imperial brow.

That is a grand kind of patience, too, when we can wait without unbelief. Two little words are good for every Christian to learn and to practice—pray and stay. Waiting on the Lord implies both praying and staying. What if the world is not converted this year! What if the Lord Jesus does not come tomorrow! What if still our tribulations are lengthened out! What if the conflict is continued! He that has been tried and by grace has obtained the true profit of his trials both quietly waits and joyfully hopes for the salvation of God. Patience, brother! Is this high virtue scarce with you? The Holy Spirit shall bestow it upon you through suffering.

Brothers and sisters, if we learn endurance, we have taken a high degree. You look at the weather-beaten sailor, the man who is at home on the sea: he has a bronzed face and mahogany-colored flesh; he looks as tough as heart of oak and as hardy as if he were made of iron. How different from us poor landsmen. How did the man become so inured to hardships, so able to breast the storm? By doing business in great waters. He could not have become a hardy seaman by tarrying on shore. Now, trial works in the saints that spiritual hardihood which cannot be learned in ease.

You may go to school forever, but you cannot learn endurance there. Strong faith and brave patience come of trouble, and a few men in the church who have thus been prepared are worth anything in time of tempest. To reach that condition of firm endurance and sacred hardihood is worth all the expense of all the heaped-up troubles that ever come upon us from above or from beneath. The Lord give us more of this choice grace.

THE SPIRITUAL COMPLETENESS PROMOTED

Lastly, all this works something better still: "That you may be perfect and complete, lacking nothing." Brethren, the most valuable thing a man can get in this world is that which has most to do with his truest self. A man gets a good house; well, that is something. But suppose he is in bad health; what is the good of his fine mansion? A man is well clothed and well fed; that is something. But suppose he shivers with ague, and has no appetite through indigestion. That spoils it all. If a man is in robust health, this is a far more valuable boon. Health is far more to be prized than wealth, or honor, or learning; we all allow that. But then suppose that a man's innermost self is diseased while his body is healthy, so that he is disgraced by vice or fevered with passion? The very best thing is that which will make the man himself a better man—make him right, and true, and pure, and holy. When the man himself is better, he has made an unquestionable gain. So, if our afflictions tend, by trying our faith, to breed patience, and that patience tends to make us into perfect men in Christ Jesus, then we may be glad of trials. Afflictions by God's grace make us all-round men, developing every spiritual faculty, and therefore they are our friends, our helpers, and should be welcomed with "all joy."

Our trials, when blessed of God to make us patient, ripen

us. I do not know how to explain what I mean by ripening, but there is a sort of mellowness about believers who have endured a great deal of affliction that you never meet in other people. It cannot be mistaken or imitated. A certain measure of sunlight is wanted to bring out the real flavor of fruits, and when a fruit has felt its measure of burning sun it develops a lusciousness which we all delight in. So is it in men and women: a certain amount of trouble appears needed to create a certain sugar of graciousness in them so that they may contain the rich, ripe juice of a gracious character.

Dear brothers and sisters, there is a certain all-roundness of spiritual manhood which never comes to us except by manifold temptations. Let me attempt to show you what I mean. Sanctified trials produce a chastened spirit. Some of us by nature are rough and untender; but after a while friends notice that the roughness is departing, and they are quite glad to be more gently handled. Ah, that sick chamber did the polishing. Under God's grace, that depression of spirit, that loss, that cross, that bereavement—these softened the natural ruggedness and made the man meek and lowly, like his Lord. Sanctified trouble has a great tendency to breed sympathy, and sympathy is to the church as oil to machinery. A man that has never suffered feels very awkward when he tries to sympathize with a tried child of God. He kindly does his best, but he does not know how to go to work at it; but those repeated blows from the rod make us feel for others who are smarting.

Have you never noticed how tried men, too, when their trouble is thoroughly sanctified, become cautious and humble? They cannot speak quite so fast as they used to do. They do not talk of being absolutely perfect, though they are the very men who are scripturally perfect. They say little about their own doings and much about the tender mercy of the Lord. They recollect the whipping they had behind the door from their Father's hands, and they speak gently to other erring ones. Affliction is the stone which our Lord Jesus throws at the brow of our giant pride, and patience is the sword which cuts off its head.

Those, too, are the kind of people who are most grateful. I have known what it is to praise God for the power to move one leg in bed. It may not seem much to you, but it was a great blessing to me. They that are heavily afflicted come to bless God for everything. Troubled men get to be grateful men, and that is no small thing. As a rule, where God's grace works, these come to be hopeful men. Where others think the storm will destroy the vessel, they can remember storms equally fierce which did not destroy it, and so they are so calm that their courage keeps others from despair.

These men, too, become unworldly men. These much-tempted ones are frequently the most spiritual men, and out of this spirituality comes usefulness. Mr. Greatheart, who led the band of pilgrims up to the celestial city, was a man of many trials, or he would not have been fit to lead so many to their heavenly rest; and you, dear brother, if ever you are to be a leader and a helper, it must be by such means as this that you must be prepared for it. Do you not wish to have every virtue developed? Do you not wish to become a perfect man in Christ Jesus? If so, welcome with all joy various trials and temptations;

fly to God with them; bless Him for having sent them. Ask Him to help you to bear them with patience, and then let that patience have its perfect work, and so by the Spirit of God you shall become "perfect and complete, lacking nothing."

TITLE:
The Present Crisis

TEXT:
Hosea 5:15

SUMMARY:
In our crisis and trials in a nation, and as believers, we can be sure that God will not cast off His people—He has decreed He will not. However, that does not mean the Lord will withhold discipline from His children. When God does withdraw, it is that we would come back to Him in repentance. To be outside of fellowship with God is life-draining upon the believer, therefore we must repent and draw nearer to God.

NOTABLE QUOTES:
"Be anxious to be reconciled to Him. Long to be at peace with the great God who made the heavens and the earth."

"When these withdrawments of God are painfully felt, then we should begin most eagerly to search out the sin which has caused them, for sin is at the bottom of it all."

"It is good to repent at once, and seek our heavenly Father's face soon."

3

The Present Crisis

I will go and return to my place,
till they acknowledge their offence, and seek my
face: in their affliction they will seek me early.

HOSEA 5:15 KJV

THE LORD DOES NOT ALWAYS TELL US what He will do. He has told us that "it is the glory of God to conceal a matter," and our Lord Jesus has said, "It is not for you to know the times or seasons which the Father has put in His own authority." When He does make known to us what He is about to do, it is not to gratify our curiosity but to direct our conduct.

In this case the Lord speaks aloud concerning His intentions. He had grown weary with chastening His people, and therefore He was about to withdraw Himself from them and leave them alone. He says, "I will go and return to my place," as if His waiting time was over, and He would no longer remain in their midst to be provoked by their obstinacy. This withdrawal would occasion the non-acceptance of their prayers and offerings. This He tells them so that they may be led to implore Him to remain with them; or that if He be already gone, they may by hearty confession of their sin, and an immediate seeking of His face, prevail upon Him once more to visit them in His grace.

If God is about to go, then all is going; even hope itself is removing. The divine departure is the worst of calamities, and therefore it is but right that those who are threatened with such a judgment should put their thoughts together and consider their ways and use the best means to hold Him or to bring Him back again before He has closed the door between Him and them. There should be an eager desire to bring the King back that once more the heart may sun itself in the light of His favor. Dear friends, I shall speak this morning with the most anxious desire to be practical, longing and praying in my heart that wherever sin has begun to separate between us and God we may be stirred up to acknowledge our offenses and to seek His face, and that where such a separation has long existed there may arise an intense desire of the whole soul to return from its banishment and draw near to God.

PRESENT NATIONAL TROUBLES

I desire to speak of these things as before God in all sincerity and simplicity. I know it is impossible to touch upon such a subject without being suspected of political bias, but I can truly declare that from all such partiality I desire to be freed, that I may not speak as a partisan but as the servant of the living

God. Calmly and solemnly would I speak words of soberness and truth and justice. It is a burden to my heart to speak a hard word of my own beloved country, and if I seem to do so it is not in wantonness but because of a pressure upon my conscience which will not let me be silent.

Surely no one will deny that our country is passing through a season of great and grievous adversity. We have been perplexed for many months, and even for years, with perpetual rumors of wars. For a long time no man knew when he went to rest at night but what the journal of the morning would inform him that our nation had plunged into war with one at least of the great powers of Europe. It is wonderful that we have escaped from embroiling ourselves in long and serious war, for many a time the flames of contention have threatened a general conflagration. This disquietude of itself has been a serious injury to the prosperity of our country, for trade and commerce make prosperous voyages upon the waters of peace, but even before those waters are disturbed by the storms of actual war, while only the threat of battle ruffles the surface, they make small headway or are driven back. Commerce is timid as a dove and is fluttered by every turmoil or whisper of coming trouble. In a thousand ways political agitations stab at the heart of national prosperity.

In addition to this we have been actually engaged in two wars at the least, wars certainly expensive and questionably expedient. In these two conflicts it was impossible for us to gain honor, since they were cases of the mighty assailing the feeble. Laurels gained from nations so far inferior to us would have been unworthy of a place upon the brow of a brave nation. We have invaded one country and then another with no better justification than the law of superior force or the suspicion of future danger. Our acts of aggression must be paid for not only with the blood of our soldiers but with the sinews and sweat of our working men. Results of industry which ought to have gone to support the arts and promote the comfort and advancement of humanity have been thrown away in wasteful feats of arms. The food which should have fed our children has been flung into the mouth of the lion, to be devoured by war, that its evil spirit may become yet more ravenous. We have meddled in many things and have threatened at least three of the great quarters of the globe either with our fleets or our armies. These wars, whatever their issue, are serious calamities.

On the back of all this war has come depression in trade. Everywhere there is complaining, and not without cause. Striving tradesmen wonder whether they shall be able to "provide things honest in the sight of all men." Many a man now plans and labors, but his care and toil earn but a scant reward. All trade is dull, and some trade is dead. The land mourns, and men's hearts sink for fear. It is a day of darkness and of gloominess, a day of clouds and of thick darkness.

As if all this were not enough, the heavens refuse to assist the processes of husbandry. For the most part the crop of hay, so needful for the cattle, may be regarded as lost, and now the great peril is upon the corn. It seems certain that a continuance of this constant rain must deprive us of the most precious fruits of the earth. Farmers are beginning to cry out bitterly, and there is a demand that prayer should be offered in all the churches for fair weather. May God be pleased to look upon our land and deliver us in this hour of trouble, for indeed it is a time of loss and ruin to thousands! If ever prayer was needed, it is surely at this hour.

In the first matter, that of a warlike policy, we may by God's goodness make a change. It may be possible that ere long better principles will come to the front, and we may no longer be made to appear as a nation of snarlers and growlers delighting in war. God grant it speedily! But as to the two other matters, what can we do? We are powerless to quicken trade; we are certainly powerless to stay the bottles of heaven. If God wills it, the clouds will gather from day to day and drench our fields with their pitiless downpour. Deluge will follow deluge till the corn shall rot in the fields if God so determines. Prayer is therefore desired, and well it may be. But by some, prayer is desired as if it were quite certain that if certain pious words are repeated the rain must necessarily cease and the weather become favorable. I am not quite so sure. Let prayer be offered, by all means, but only under certain conditions can it prove effectual. I know of many reasons why it may be possible that such prayers as are likely to be offered will not be heard, but instead thereof the threatened judgment of God may nevertheless come upon us.

I desire, this morning, to speak about prayer in the way of warning, lest men should place an unwise confidence in the formality of reading a form of prayer in churches or uttering extempore formalities in meetinghouses. Few men believe more thoroughly in the power of real prayer than I do, and I have tested and proved it in many remarkable ways so fully that I can have no doubts as to its efficacy. But still we must use our understandings, lest we be deceived, and come to expect what we shall not receive. I would call to your recollection the fact that, under certain circumstances, God does not answer prayer. Our text says, "I will go and return to my place, till they acknowledge their offence." If this be the case, there will be no answering of prayer till repentance is manifested.

Sometimes the heavens are brass, and their cries reverberate and come back into their own ears, not without a blessing to themselves, but still without any visible reply as to the people for whom their intercessions were offered. It is not every sort of prayer that God will hear, for He says by His servant Isaiah, "When you spread out your hands, I will hide My eyes from you; Even though you make many prayers, I will not hear. Your hands are full of blood." Intercession is sometimes useless, for Jeremiah tells us, "Even if Moses and Samuel stood before Me, My mind would not be favorable toward this people." David, doubtless, prayed earnestly that he might escape from the chastisement of his sin when he numbered the people, but it could not be removed. He had a choice of three evils, but one of the three was inevitable. When God has come to this pass with a people, that He must and will smite them, prayer is their only resource, and even that may fail to avert the threatened stroke. I pray to God that the rain may cease, but if it should be continued, it will not be because the Lord cannot help us or has ceased to answer prayer.

Remember, too, that not only may God withdraw Himself in anger, but it may be His determination to punish a people out of a far-seeing design for their good. Perhaps, as a nation, we have had too much prosperity. Ease and plenty have begotten pride and luxury, and these may have weakened the spirit of the nation. It may have become absolutely necessary for this favored nation, if it is to be still the stronghold of liberty and the fortress of gospel truth, that it should again endure those northern blasts of adversity which have aforetime strengthened it at heart. It will not be the first time that our land has suffered for her good.

I would not wish ill to my country, but if our fellow men will not remember God except in adversity, adversity itself might be desired by the kindest heart. If true religion is to be cast into the dust by boastful infidelity, if a bastard popery is to be allowed to occupy our national churches, if drunkenness is to remain shameless and almost universal, if the language of the common people is to become filthy and obscene, if the exaltation of one favored sect above its fellow Christians is to be perpetually to endure, if our nation is to shed the blood of weaker nations and send its armies into lands which are none of ours, then it will not be a strange thing if the Lord resolves to punish, and it will be hard for the righteous man to find an argument with which to plead for pity.

Can we expect pardon on other terms? Can we even ask for it? The verdict of the sternly just would rather be "Let the rod fall" than "Let it be withdrawn" if only by severe means the nation can be made to put away its evil deeds. In our text God declares that He will not give audience to His erring people but will retire into His secret place until they acknowledge the offense and seek His face. It may be so with our nation at this time, and if it be we need to be exhorted to something more than public prayer. There is need of a work more thorough and more difficult than the public use of a devotional form.

But, says one, "We hope we shall have national prayer." I hope so too, but will there be a national confession of sin? If not, how can mere prayer avail? Will there be a general desire to do that which is just and right? Will that be a declaration that England's policy is never to trample on the weak or pick a quarrel for her own aggrandizement? Will there be a loathing of the principle that British interests are to be our guiding star instead of justice and right? Personal interests are no excuse for doing wrong; if they were so we should have to exonerate the worst of thieves, for they will not invade a house until their personal interests invite them. Perhaps the midnight robber may yet learn to plead that he only committed a burglary for fear another thief should take the spoil and make worse use of it than he.

When our own interests are our policy, nobility is dead and true honor is departed, but I fear that only a minority are of this mind. Will the nation repent of any one of its sins? Will it settle itself down like the people of Jerusalem during the great rain of Ezra's time and do that which is right in the sight of God? If stern reformation went with supplication, I am persuaded that prayer would prevail; but while sin is gloried in, my hopes find little ground to rest upon.

But will there be general prayer? No, there will not. I speak sadly, but I speak no more than the truth. There are numbers among us who say that prayer is of no use with regard to the winds and the clouds, for certain laws govern the weather, and prayer cannot affect those laws. These men, therefore, will not pray, and there are multitudes of others of like spirit whose atheism is practical though it is unavowed. How, then, can prayer be general when such vast numbers utterly disregard it? Turn your eyes to Nineveh. When Jonah threatened that great city, and upon its repentance the judgment was withdrawn, of what character was its humiliation? From the king on the throne even to the beasts in the field, all were clothed with sackcloth, and fasted, and cried out to God, and therefore we marvel not that He heard them. Will there be any such crying to God among us? I think not. A defiant silence will seal millions of lips.

But what of those who are supposed to pray? Are all these men of the Elias stamp, whose fervent prayer could open or shut the windows of heaven? We dare not put much confidence in the prayers which will be offered. Will they be offered in faith by a tenth of those who will repeat them? I wish I could hope so. By many the public prayer will be regarded as absolutely ridiculous, and by many more as a mere matter of form.

What then is to be done? This much is to be done. All hope for a country lies in the true believers who dwell therein. Remember Sodom, and how it would have been spared had there been ten righteous men found, and know that you also are the salt of the earth, by whom it is to be conserved. Loathe the spirit of those who say that, because we are citizens of heaven, we are to have nothing to do with the concerns of men below. A more un-Christianlike sentiment, a more selfish sentiment, never degraded spiritual minds. Wherever the Jews dwelt in the days of their scattering they were commanded to care for the good of the people among whom they dwelt. Here are the words of the Lord by Jeremiah: "Seek the peace of the city where I have caused you to be carried away captive, and pray to the Lord for it; for in its peace you will have peace." Surely Christians are not to be less generous than Jews. You cannot shirk your responsibility anyhow except by clearing out of the land altogether, and then if it suffers by your absence you will still be found guilty. You are part and parcel of the nation, for you share in its protection and privileges, and it is yours as Christian men to feel that you are bound in return to do all you can in the midst of it to promote truth and righteousness.

What then? What course should we now pursue? Let us make confession of sin on behalf of the people as Moses and Jeremiah and Daniel did aforetime. You may not consider that to be sin which I judge to be so, but, my brother, you see sin enough all around you of one sort or another. Take it to yourself, and as the high priest went in to the holy place to plead for the people, so act you as a priest before God in your quiet personal devotions. Confess the sin of this nation before God. If it will not repent, repent for it. Stand as a sort of consecrated sponsor before God, and let the sin lie on your heart till you fall on your face before the Most High. Remember, the saints are intercessors with God for the people. Get you up to your Carmels [1 Kings 18] and cry aloud, you that know how to cry unto God, that He may send deliverance, and when you have prayed for this people and asked the Lord to forgive its sin, and also to take away the chastising rod, then all of you promote by your daily lives, your precepts, and your actions, "whatever things are true, whatever things are noble, whatever things are just, whatever things are pure, whatever things are lovely, whatever things are of good report." Love God and your fellow men and seek to promote all interests which look that way.

I believe that a country can never have a larger blessing, a truer safeguard for the present, or a firmer security for its future greatness, than a band of praying men and women who make mention of it before the throne of God.

Thus have I spoken what was burdening my heart; make what you will of it; it is the warning of an honest lover of his country who fears the Lord and fears none besides. Judge me to have spoken with political bias or not, and censure me as you choose. I could say no less, or I would gladly have held my peace. Before God I am clear in this thing of any attempt but an upright one. May God grant that my feeble protest may touch the hearts of those who ought to feel its truth. I am not very sanguine that it will be so, for we have fallen upon evil times, and the heart of the people has waxen gross.

OUR PERSONAL TRIALS

Brethren and sisters, let us now commune with one another concerning the ways of God with our own souls. The Lord will not cast off His people; notwithstanding their faults, they are His own children, and they shall be His children forever. But when His children sin, God is sure to chasten them for it. He leaves His enemies alone for a while, but He smites His sons.

His foes shall go unpunished till the end shall be; but as for His beloved, He is exceedingly jealous over them, and He will make them smart when they sin. Has the Lord been chastening any of us of late? Has the moth been in our estates, or has the lion been tearing our peace? Let us turn at His rebuke. It is good to repent at once and seek our heavenly Father's face soon.

For, note next, when chastisements are of no avail, withdrawment follows. The Lord has promised that He will not forsake His people, nor will He utterly do so, but there are withdrawments which are not included in that promise. God may so hide Himself from His servants that they may have no conscious fellowship with Him, no enjoyment of His word, no power in prayer. In fact, they may pray and He may shut out their prayer. Their life may be sapless and spiritless; joy and peace may flee. They may possibly try at such times to make up for their loss by enjoying the world. They are spoiled for such empty vanities. Grace has made them incapable of finding soul food in the corn and wine of earth. They must have their God or die. Let me tell you most solemnly that it is a very sad thing when God has withdrawn from a believing spirit, and the more holy a man has been the more sadly will he lament that he is now under a cloud.

When these withdrawments of God are painfully felt, then we should begin most eagerly to search out the sin which has caused them, for sin is at the bottom of it all. If, believer, there be a quarrel between your Beloved and yourself, is there not a cause? Our Lord Jesus is no fitful lover who will leave the soul espoused to Him merely to indulge a whim. Far otherwise; He never trifles with us but treats our love as a sacred thing.

There is some grave cause whenever the Beloved frowns.

Now for a thorough search, a sweeping of the house, and a cleansing out of all things that offend. Throughout the heart, the understanding, and the lips let a search warrant be issued, and if any sin be detected, let it be brought to light and judged. Set it in the light of God's countenance and there confess it and lament it. Make no apologies, excuses, and explanations, but honestly confess the wrong and leave it. Bring the idols out and let your heart see the wounds they have given you, and what it is that you have doted on, and what these things are which have come in between you and your God. Surely you will be ashamed of them when you consider that their love is the price for which you have parted with your Savior's presence. Judas's pieces of silver were not more contemptible than these poor paltry bribes. Lament the treachery of your heart.

But, beloved, when you have obtained a sense of the sin or sins which separate you from God, and have made a full confession, then take care that you seek the Lord with hopefulness and confidence, for, notwithstanding all this, you are His child still and must not give way to a paralyzing despair. You are married unto Christ, and there is no divorce with Him. He will not cast off forever nor put away His erring spouse. Come, therefore, unto Him with humble confidence. He has torn and He will heal; He has smitten and He will bind us up. Seek His face, for His face is toward you.

The very face of God is Jesus Christ. The Son of God is He in whom we see the Father. Even as you see a man in his countenance, so God is seen in Christ. Seek God in Christ Jesus, for thereby good shall come unto you. He will not reject you. You are not out of reach of His love; He will turn again and have compassion on you, for He delights in mercy. If He withdraws, it is only that you may sigh after Him and seek after Him. He is very near us all the while, and He will yet be found of us. O backslider, Jesus waits to be gracious to you. He longs to restore you. Only acknowledge your transgression and return to Him. Be of good cheer as to acceptance, for He casts out none who come to Him. End these backslidings, and there need be no more misery. God help you to rise this very day into a closer walk with Him, and may He keep you by His side forever.

To be out of fellowship with God is for the heart to be in a state of spiritual disease. Things must be wrong within when we are wrong with God. When we do not walk in the light, as God is in the light, there is some evil in the eye of the soul. Dread the evil, and cry for healing.

To be away from God is to be in a state of spiritual weakness. Samson may shake himself as at other times, but he can do no deeds of strength when the Lord has departed from him. God is our strength, and God's hiding makes us weak as water. If the Lord should leave us, we cannot plead with Him and prevail, nor can we plead with men and win them for Christ. Our strength has departed, both toward God and toward man, when our fellowship with God is suspended. Our heart cannot leap like a young roe upon the mountains, but our spirit limps as one whose bones are broken. We cannot even gaze through the gates of pearl to see the glory which the Spirit reveals, for our eye is dim, so that we cannot see afar off when Jesus is away.

If you are in this condition, you are in an evil case; burdensome care invades you, anxieties annoy you, your temper gets the mastery, Satan accuses, and conscience trembles. Your spirit is like that of a carnal man, and you are apt to speak unadvisedly with your lips and to be readily moved by every external influence. What is worse, when a man is out of fellowship with God, he is in danger of presumptuous sins. David on the terraces of his palace had not been walking with God, or else the sight of Bathsheba below had not caused him so grievous a fall. Lose communion with Christ, and you are on the verge of a folly which will stain your character and terribly mar your life.

It is only when we are near to God that we are safe; therefore, let a sense of danger drive us to Him at once. I speak from a widespread observation as well as from an inward experience: there is but a step between distance from God and the nearness of temptation and sin. If God thinks much of you, He will have you near Him, or else He will make you miserable. He will not permit you to rejoice except in Himself. If your love is not worth His having, you may love whom you like, but when He loves you much He will be very jealous over you, and if He finds you are content to be without His company, He will make you suffer for such wantonness and ingratitude.

That bypath meadow business, that going down the green lane to get off the flints of the right road, that getting away from Christ to have a taste of the world's sweet delusions, that coming down from our high places as if we had grown weary of being happy, and were discontented with an angelic life— all that means a succession of afflictions and regrets which can only at the very best end in our getting to Christ again with broken bones. Such wanderings are painful, end how they may.

David's career before his sin, how different it was from his life afterwards. You can always tell which psalms he wrote before his transgression; they are so jubilant, so full of holy rejoicing. But afterwards when he sings, it is in a bass voice; he loves his God, but it is the solemn, tearful love of repentance rather than the bright sparkling love of delight in God. Do not err, my beloved brethren, for error brings sorrow.

PERSONAL TRIALS OF THE SINNER

Oh, you that are unconverted, if God means to save you, He will before long begin by chastening you in body or in mind. You will have trouble. You are a wandering sheep, and God will send His black dog after you to fetch you to the fold. If one trouble does not do it, you will have another, and another, and another. Perhaps I speak to some who, as the result of providential chastenings and the work of conscience on their spirit, have already been aroused; let them take heed of trifling with their awakenings. After that earnest sermon, or after reading that stirring book, you did begin to pray, but your desires and feelings have now subsided. I would have you greatly grieve over this. Let me warn you that God may withdraw Himself from you altogether. This is a more terrible calamity than you suspect; unless it be averted it will be your ruin.

I may be speaking to some strangers here who at one time had a disturbed conscience, but they have grown very callous of late. It is high time for you to seek the Lord. When you were smitten before, you tried self-righteousness, churchgoing, chapel going, sacraments, and so forth. You must now return to your God, or you will never be right. It is vain to look to priests, or sacraments, or religiousnesses: all these things put together are nothing. You must have personal dealings with your God, and you must confess your sin to Him, or you will be eternally undone. Go and do it this morning.

Be anxious to be reconciled to Him. Long to be at peace with the great God who made the heavens and the earth. Why should there be a quarrel between your Creator and your soul? The way of reconciliation is by the blood of His Son Jesus Christ. You must, therefore, trust Jesus, and you shall find the peace of God. Oh may His Spirit help you to do this now. Seek Him, and seek Him intensely, resolving that you will never cease to seek till you find God full of mercy and love to you. Come, I pray you, and turn to the Lord now, and may the Holy Spirit aid you in so doing. He has torn and He will heal you. He has smitten and He will bind you up.

God Himself must heal you, or you will never be healed. He who has broken your heart must give you comfort, or you will never have any. Hasten to your chamber at once, and then upon your knees cry out unto God with the prayer of faith. Be not content with your own sense of sin. No, your sense of sin may be but the first drop of a shower of eternal remorse. Get away to God in Christ, and rest not till you are there. He made you, and you cannot be happy without Him. While He is angry with you, you cannot be at peace. He bids you come to Him. The smitings of His providence are meant to separate you from the love of sin and drive you to your God. Believe in Jesus and live. God bless you, my beloved friends, for His name's sake. Amen.

TITLE:
For the Troubled

TEXT:
Psalm 88:7

SUMMARY:
In the middle of trial, the tried Christian must be swift to the Scriptures for endurance, for all Christians err in the direction of overrating their troubles. We can easily mislead our souls into believing God is wrathful toward us, that we experience the hatred of God. We must remember that it is Christ who has borne our justified wrath. We must remember the sanctifying work of the trials God puts in our paths—they bring God glory and form us into the image of the Son.

NOTABLE QUOTES:
"We pray to be like Christ, but how can we be if we are not men of sorrows at all and never become the acquaintance of grief?"

"Do not let us expect when we are in the trouble to perceive any immediate benefit resulting from it."

"Now, child of God, if you are suffering today in any way whatever, whether from the ills of poverty or bodily sickness, or depression of spirits, recollect there is not a drop of the judicial anger of God in it all."

4

For the Troubled

Your wrath lies heavy upon me,
and You have afflicted me with all Your waves.

PSALM 88:7

IT IS THE BUSINESS OF A SHEPHERD not only to look
after the happy among the sheep but to seek after the sick of
the flock and to lay himself out right earnestly for their comfort
and succor. I feel, therefore, that I do rightly when I make it my
special business to speak to such as are in trouble. Those of you
who are happy and rejoicing in God, full of faith and assurance,
can very well spare a discourse for your weaker brethren. You
can be even glad and thankful to go without your portion, that
those who are depressed in spirit may receive a double measure
of the wine of consolation. Moreover, I am not sure that even
the most joyous Christian is any the worse for remembering
the days of darkness which are stealing on apace, "for they are
many." Just as the memories of our dying friends come o'er us
like a cloud, so will the recollection that there are tribulations

and afflictions in the world sober our rejoicing and prevent its degenerating into an idolatry of the things of time and sense. It is better for many reasons to go to the house of mourning than to the house of feasting. It may be, you who are today brimming with happiness, that a little store of sacred cautions and consolations may prove no sore to you. This morning's discourse upon sorrow may suggest a few thoughts to you which, being treasured up, shall ripen like summer fruit and mellow by the time your winter shall come round.

It is clear to all those who read the narratives of Scripture, or are acquainted with good men, that the best of God's servants may be brought into the very lowest estate. There is no promise of present prosperity appointed to true religion. As men, the people of God share the common lot of men, and what is that but trouble? Yea, there are some sorrows which are peculiar to Christians, though these are something more than balanced by those peculiar and bitter troubles which belong to the ungodly, from which the Christian is delivered.

From the passage which is open before us, we learn that sons of God may be brought so low as to write and sing psalms which are sorrowful throughout and have no fitting accompaniment but sighs and groans. They do not often do so, but sometimes saints are forced to sing such dolorous ditties that from beginning to end there is not one note of joy. Yet even in their dreariest winter night, the saints have an aurora in their sky, and in this, the dreariest of all psalms, there is a faint gleam in the first verse, like a star falling upon its threshold—"O LORD, God of my salvation."

Heman [the Ezrahite] retained his hold upon his God. It is not all darkness in a heart which can cry, "My God," and the child of God, however low he may sink, still keeps hold upon his God. "Though He slay me, yet will I trust in him," is the resolution of his soul. Jehovah smites me, but He is my God. He frowns upon me, but He is my God. He tramples me into the very dust, and lays me in the lowest pit, as among the dead, yet still He is my God, and such will I call Him till I die; even when He leaves me I will cry, "My God, My God, why have You forsaken Me?"

Moreover, the believer in his worst time still continues to pray, and prays, perhaps, the more vigorously because of his sorrows. God's rod flogs His child not from Him, but to Him. Our griefs are waves which wash us to the rock. This psalm is full of prayer; it is as much sweetened with supplication as it is salted with sorrow. Now, while a man can pray he is never far from light; he is at the window, though, perhaps, as yet the curtains are not drawn aside. The man who can pray has the clue in his hand by which to escape from the labyrinth of affliction. Like the trees in winter, we may say of the praying man, when his heart is greatly troubled, "his substance is in him, though he has lost his leaves."

Prayer is the soul's breath, and if it breathes it lives, and, living, it will gather strength again. A man must have true and eternal life within him while he can continue still to pray, and while there is such life there is assured hope. Still the best child of God may be the greatest sufferer, and his sufferings may appear to be crushing, killing, and overwhelming.

They may also be so very protracted as to attend him all his days, and their bitterness may be intense, all of which, and much more, this mournful psalm teaches us.

EXPOSITION

In the first place, its strong language suggests the remark that tried saints are prone to overrate their afflictions. I believe we all err in that direction. The inspired man of God who wrote our text was touched with this common infirmity, for he overstates his case. Read his words, "Your wrath lies heavy upon me." I have no doubt Heman meant wrath in its worst sense. He believed that God was really angry with him, and wrathful with him, even as He is with the ungodly; but that was not true. As we shall show, there is a very grave difference between the anger of God with His children and the anger of God with His enemies. We do not think Heman sufficiently discerned that difference, even as we are afraid that many of God's children even now forget it and therefore fear that the Lord is punishing them according to strict justice. Ah, if poor bewildered believers could but see it, they would learn that the very thing which they call wrath is only love, in its own wise manner, seeking their highest good.

Besides, the psalmist says, "Your wrath lies heavy upon me." Ah, if Heman had known what it was to have God's wrath lie hard on him, he would have withdrawn that word, for all the wrath that any man ever feels in this life is but as a laying on of God's little finger. It is in the world to come that the wrath of God lies heavy on men. Here the really sore pressure of wrath is not known, and especially not known by a child of God. It is too strong a speech if we weigh it in the scales of sober truth. It outruns the fact, even though it were the most sorrowful living man that uttered it.

Then Heman adds, "You have afflicted me with all Your waves," as though he were a wreck with the sea breaking over him, and the whole ocean, and all the oceans, were running full against him as the only object of their fury. But it was not so. All God's waves have broken over no man, save only the Son of Man. There are still some troubles which we have been spared, some woes to us unknown. Are there not modes of pain from which our bodies have escaped? Are there not also some mental pangs which have not wrung our spirit? And what if we seem to have traversed the entire circle of bodily and mental misery, yet in our homes, households, or friendships we have surely some comfort left, and therefore from some rough billow we are screened.

Among the living, none can literally know what all God's waves would be. They know, who are condemned to feel the blasts of His indignation, they know in the land of darkness and of everlasting hurricane; they know what all God's waves and billows are, but we know not. The metaphor is good and admirable, and correct enough poetically, but as a statement of fact it is strained.

We are all apt to aggravate our grief. I say this here as a general fact, but I would not vex the sick man with it while he is enduring the weight of his affliction. If he can calmly accept the suggestion of his own accord, it may do him good, but it would be cruel to throw it at him. True as it is, I should not like to whisper it in any sufferer's ear, because it would not console but grieve him. I have often marveled at the strange comfort persons offer you when they say, "Ah, there are others who suffer more than you do." Am I expected to rejoice at the news of other people's miseries? Far otherwise, I am pained to think there should be sharper smarts than mine. I can conceive of a fiend in torment finding solace in the belief that others are tortured with a yet fiercer flame, but surely such diabolical comfort should not be offered to Christian men.

There is, however, a form of comfort akin to it, but of far more legitimate origin, a consolation honorable and divine. There was One upon whom God's wrath pressed very sorely, One who was in truth afflicted with all God's waves, and that One is our brother, a man like ourselves, the dearest lover of our souls; and because He has known and suffered all this, He can enter into sympathy with us this morning whatever tribulation may beat upon us. His passion is all over now, but not His compassion. He has borne the indignation of God and turned it all away from us. As we think of Him, the Crucified, our souls may not only derive consolation from His sympathy and powerful succor, but we may learn to look upon our trials with a calmer eye and judge them more according to the true standard. In the presence of Christ's cross our own crosses are less colossal. Our thorns in the flesh are as nothing when laid side by side with the nails and spear.

But, secondly, let us remark that saints do well to trace all their trials to their God. Heman did so in the text: "Your wrath lies heavy upon me, You have afflicted me with all Your waves." He traces all his adversity to the Lord his God. It is God's wrath, they are God's waves that afflict him, and God makes them afflict him. Child of God, never forget this: all that you are suffering of any sort comes to you from the divine hand. Truly, you say, "my affliction arises from wicked men," yet remember that there is a predestination which, without soiling the fingers of the Infinitely Holy, nevertheless rules the motions of evil men as well as of holy angels. It were a dreary thing for us if there were no appointments of God's providence which concerned the ungodly. Then the great mess of mankind would be entirely left to chance, and the godly might be crushed by them without hope. The Lord, without interfering with the freedom of their wills, rules and overrules, so that the ungodly are as a rod in His hand with which He wisely scourges His children.

Perhaps you will say that your trials have arisen not from the sins of others, but from your own sin. Even then I would have you penitently trace them still to God. What though the trouble spring out of the sin, yet it is God that has appointed the sorrow to follow the transgression, to act as a remedial agency for your spirit. Look not at the second cause, or, looking at it with deep regret, turn your eye chiefly to your heavenly Father, and "hear ye the rod, and who hath appointed it." The Lord sends upon us the evil as well as the good of this mortal life. His is the sun that cheers and the frost that chills, His the deep calm, and His the fierce tornado. To dwell on second causes is frequently frivolous, a sort of solemn trifling.

Men say of each affliction, "It might have been prevented if so and so had occurred." Perhaps if another physician had been called in, the dear child's life had still been spared; possibly if I had moved in such a direction in business, I might not have been a loser. Who is to judge what might have been? In endless conjectures we are lost, and, cruel to ourselves, we gather material for unnecessary griefs. Matters happened not so; then why conjecture what would have been had things been different? It is folly. You did your best, and it did not answer; why rebel? To fix the eye upon the second cause will irritate the mind. We grow indignant with the more immediate agent of our grief, and so fail to submit ourselves to God. Brother, forgive the man who injured you—his was the sin, forgive it, as you hope to be forgiven; but yours is the chastisement, and it comes from God, therefore endure it and ask grace to profit by it. The more we get away from intermediate agents the better, for when we reach to God, grace will make submission easy.

But now, thirdly, afflicted children of God do well to have a keen eye to the wrath that mingles with their troubles. "Your wrath lies heavy upon me." There is Heman's first point. He does not mention the waves of affliction till he has first spoken of the wrath. We should labor to discover what the Lord means by smiting us, what He purposes by the chastisement, and how far we can answer that purpose. We must use a keen eye clearly to distinguish things.

There is an anger and an anger, a wrath and a wrath. God is never angry with His children in one sense, but He is in another. As men, we have all of us disobeyed the laws of God, and God stands in relationship to all of us as a judge. As a judge, He must execute upon us the penalties of His law, and He must, from the necessity of His nature, be angry with us for having broken that law. That concerns all the human race. But the moment a man believes in the Lord Jesus Christ his offenses are his offenses no longer; they are laid upon Christ Jesus, the substitute, and the anger goes with the sin. The anger of God toward the sins of believers has spent itself upon Christ. Christ has been punished in their stead; the punishment due to their sin has been borne by Jesus Christ. God forbid that the Judge of all the earth should ever be unjust. It were not just for God to punish a believer for a sin which has been already laid upon Jesus Christ. Hence the believer is altogether free from all liability to suffer the judicial anger of God and all risk of receiving a punitive sentence from the Most High. The man is absolved—shall he be judged again? The man has paid the debt—shall he be brought a second time before the judge, as though he were still a debtor?

Now, then, the Christian man takes up another position; he is adopted into the family of God. He has become God's child. He is under the law of God's house. There is in every house an economy, a law by which the children and servants are ruled. If the child of God breaks the law of the house, the Father will visit his offense with fatherly stripes—a very different kind of visitation from that of a judge. Wide as the poles asunder are the anger of a judge and the anger of a father. The father loves the child while he is angry and is mainly angry for that very reason. If it were not his child, he would probably take no notice of its fault, but because it is his own boy who has spoken an untruth or committed an act of disobedience, he feels he must chastise him because he loves him. This needs no further explanation.

There is a righteous anger in God's heart towards guilty impenitent men; He feels none of that towards His people. He is their Father, and if they transgress, He will visit them with stripes, not as a legal punishment, since Christ has borne all that, but as a gentle paternal chastisement, that they may see their folly and repent of it and may turn unto their Father and amend their ways.

Now, child of God, if you are suffering today in any way whatever, whether from the ills of poverty or bodily sickness, or depression of spirits, recollect there is not a drop of the judicial anger of God in it all. You are not being punished for your sins as a judge punishes a culprit; never believe such false doctrine. Gospel doctrine tells us that our sins were numbered on the Great Scapegoat's head of old and carried away once for all, never to be charged against us again.

But we must use the eye of our judgment in looking at our present affliction to see and confess how richly, as children, we deserve the rod. Go back to the time since you were converted, dear brother and sister, and consider: do you wonder that God has chastened you? Speaking for myself, I wonder that I have ever escaped the rod at any time. How ungrateful have we been, how unloving, and how unlovable, how false to our holiest vows, how unfaithful to our most sacred consecrations. Is there a single ordinance over which we have not sinned? Did we ever rise from our knees without having offended while at prayer? Did we ever get through a hymn without some wandering of mind or coldness of heart? Did we ever read a chapter which we might not have wept over, because we did not receive the truth in the love of it into our soul as we ought to have done? O, good Father, if we smart, richly do we deserve that we should yet smart again. When you have confessed your sin, let me exhort you to use those same eyes zealously to search out the particular sin which has caused the present chastisement.

I do not wonder that some Christians suffer; I should wonder if they did not. I have seen them, for instance, neglect family prayer and other household duties, and their sons have grown up to dishonor them. If they cry out, "What an affliction!" we would not like to say, "Ah, but you might have expected it; you were the cause of it," but such a saying would be true. When children have left the parental roof and gone into sin, we have not been surprised when the father has been harsh, sour, and crabbed in temper. We did not expect to gather figs of thorns or grapes of thistles. We have seen men whose whole thought was "get money, get money," and yet they have professed to be Christians. Such persons have been fretful and unhappy, but we have not been astonished. Would you have the Lord deal liberally with such surly curmudgeons? Brother, the roots of your troubles may run under your doorstep where your sin lies. Search and look.

But sometimes the cause of the chastisement lies further off. Every surgeon will tell you that there are diseases which become troublesome in the prime of life, or in old age, which may have been occasioned in youth by some wrongdoing, or by accident, and the evil may have lain latent all those years. So may the sins of our youth bring upon us the sorrows of our riper years, and faults and omissions of twenty years ago may scourge us today. If the fault may be of so great an age, it should lead us to more thorough search and more frequent prayer. Perhaps when you were young you were very untender toward persons of a sorrowful spirit; you are such yourself now—your harshness is visited upon you. It may be that, when in better circumstances, you were inclined to look down upon the poor and despise the needy; your pride is chastened now. Many a minister has helped to injure another by believing a bad report against him, and by-and-by he has himself been the victim of slander.

God will visit His children's transgressions. He will frequently let common sinners go on throughout life unrebuked, but not so His children. If you were going home today and saw a number of boys throwing stones and breaking windows, you might not interfere with them, but if you saw your own lad among them, I will be bound you would fetch him out and make him repent of it. If God sees sinners going on in their evil ways, He may not punish them now—He will deal out justice to them in another state; but if it be one of His own elect, He will be sure to make him rue the day.

Perhaps the chastisement may be sent by reason of a sin as yet undeveloped, some latent proneness to evil. The grief may be meant to unearth the sin, that you may hunt it down. Have you any idea of what a devil you are by nature? None of us know what we are capable of if left by grace. We think we have a sweet temper, an amiable disposition! We shall see! We fall into provoking company, and are so teased and insulted and so cleverly touched in our raw places that we become mad with wrath and our amiable temper vanishes in smoke. Is it not a dreadful thing to be so stirred up? Yes, it is, but if our hearts were pure no sort of stirring would pollute them.

It may be a great gain to a man to know what sin is in him, for then he will humble himself before his God and begin to combat his propensities. If he had never seen the filth, he would never have swept the house. If he had never felt the pain, the disease would have lurked within, but now that he feels the pain he will fly to the remedy. Sometimes, therefore, trial may be sent that we may discern the sin which dwells in us and may seek its destruction. What shall we do this morning if we are under the smitings of God's hand, but humble ourselves before Him and go as guilty ones desiring to confess most thoroughly the particular sin which may have driven Him to chastise, appealing to the precious blood of Jesus for pardon and to the Holy Spirit for power to overcome our sin?

When you have so done let me give one word of caution before I leave this point. Do not let us expect when we are in the trouble to perceive any immediate benefit resulting from it. I have tried myself when under sharp pain to see whether I have grown a bit more resigned or more earnest in prayer or more rapt in fellowship with God, and I have never been able to see the slightest trace of improvement at such times, for pain distracts and scatters the thoughts. The gardener takes his knife and prunes the fruit trees to make them bring forth more fruit. His little child comes trudging at his heels and cries, "Father, I do not see that the fruit comes on the trees after you have cut them." No, dear child, it is not likely you would, but come round in a few months when the season of fruit has come, and then shall you see the golden apples which thank the knife. Graces which are meant to endure require time for their production.

THE BENEFITS OF TROUBLE

Many a volume has been written upon it, and it might suffice to repeat the catalogue of the benefits of trial, but I will not so detain you. Severe trouble in a true believer has the effect of loosening the roots of his soul earthward and tightening the anchor hold of his heart heavenward. How can he love the world which has become so drear to him? Why should he seek after grapes so bitter to his taste? Should he not now ask for the wings of a dove that he may fly away to his own dear country and be at rest forever?

Affliction frequently opens truths to us, and opens us to the truth—I know not which of these two is the more difficult. Experience unlocks truths which else were closed against us. Many passages of Scripture will never be made clear by the commentator; they must be expounded by experience. Many a text is written in a secret ink which must be held to the fire of adversity to make it visible. I have heard that you see stars in a well when none are visible above ground, and I am sure you can discern many a starry truth when you are down in the deeps of trouble which would not be visible to you elsewhere. Besides, I said it opened us to the truth as well as the truth to us. We are superficial in our beliefs; we are often drenched with truth, and yet it runs off from us like water from a marble slab. But affliction, as it were, ploughs us and opens up our hearts so that into our innermost nature the truth penetrates and soaks like rain into plowed land. Blessed is that man who receives the truth of God into his inmost self; he shall never lose it.

Affliction, when sanctified by the Holy Spirit, brings much glory to God out of Christians, through their experience of the Lord's faithfulness to them. We must be tried or we cannot magnify the faithful God, who will not leave His people.

Again, affliction gives us through grace the inestimable privilege of conformity to the Lord Jesus. We pray to be like Christ, but how can we be if we are not men of sorrows at all and never become the acquaintance of grief? Like Christ, and yet never traverse through the vale of tears! Like Christ, and yet have all that heart could wish and never bear the contradiction of sinners against yourself and never say, "My soul is exceedingly sorrowful, even to death." A share of His sorrow must precede a share of His glory. O, if we are ever to be like Christ, to dwell with Him eternally, we may be well content to pass through much tribulation in order to attain to it.

Once more, our sufferings are of great service to us when God blesses them, for they help us to be useful to others. It must be a terrible thing for a man never to have suffered physical pain. You say, "I should like to be the man." Ah, unless you had extraordinary grace, you would grow hard and cold, you would get to be a sort of cast-iron man, breaking other people with your touch. No, let my heart be tender, even be soft, if it must be softened by pain, for I would fain know how to bind up my fellow's wound. Let mine eye have a tear ready for my brother's sorrows even if in order to do that I should have to shed ten thousand for mine own. An escape from suffering would be an escape from the power to sympathize, and that were to be deprecated beyond all things. Luther was right when he said affliction was the best book in the minister's library. How can the man of God sympathize with the afflicted ones, if he knows nothing at all about their troubles?

If the man of God who is to minister to others could be always robust, it were perhaps a loss. If he could be always sickly, it might be equally so. But for the pastor to be able to range through all the places where the Lord suffers His sheep to go is doubtless to the advantage of His flock. And what it is to ministers, that it will be to each one of you, according to his calling, for the consolation of the people of God.

Be thankful, then, dear brethren; be thankful for trouble. Above all be thankful because it will soon be over, and we shall be in the land where these things will be spoken of with great joy. As soldiers show their scars and talk of battles when they come at last to spend their old age in the country at home, so shall we in the dear land to which we are hastening speak of the goodness and faithfulness of God which brought us through all the trials of the way. I would not like to stand in that white-robed host and hear it said, "These are they that come out of great tribulation, all except that one." Would you like to be there to see yourself pointed at as the one saint who never knew a sorrow? O no, for you would be an alien in the midst of the sacred brotherhood. We will be content to share the battle, for we shall soon wear the crown and wave the palm.

I know while I am preaching some of you have said, "Ah, these people of God have a hard time of it." So have you. The ungodly do not escape from sorrow by their sin. I never heard of a man escaping from poverty through being a spendthrift. I never heard of a man who escaped from headache or heartache by drunkenness, or from bodily pain by licentiousness. I have heard the opposite, and if there be griefs to the holy there are others for you.

Only mark this, ungodly ones. For you these things work no good. You pervert them to mischief, but for the saints they work eternal benefit. For you your sorrows are punishments; for you they are the first drops of the red hail that shall fall upon you forever. They are not so to the child of God. You are punished for your transgressions, and he is not. And let us tell you, too, that if this day you happen to be in peace, prosperity, plenty, and happiness—yet there is not one child of God here in the very deeps of trouble that would change places with you under any consideration whatever. He would sooner be God's dog and be kicked under the table than be the devil's darling and sit at meat with him.

Do you think we love God for what we get out of Him, and for nothing else? Is that your notion of a Christian's love to God? This is how the ungodly talk, and that is what the devil thought was Job's case. The devil does not understand real love and affection, but the child of God can tell the devil to his face that he loves God if He covers him with sores and sets him on the dunghill, and by God's good help he means to cling to God through troubles tenfold heavier than those he has had to bear, should they come upon him. Is He not a blessed God? Ay, let the beds of our sickness ring with it: He is a blessed God. In the night watches, when we are weary and our brain is hot and fevered and our soul is distracted, we yet confess that He is a blessed God. Every ward of the hospital where believers are found should echo with that note. A blessed God? "Ay, that He is," say the poor and needy here this morning, and so say all God's poor throughout all the land. A blessed God? "Ay," say His dying people, "as He slays us we will bless His name. He loves us, and we love Him; and, though all His waves go over us, and His wrath lies sore upon us, we would not change with kings on their thrones if they are without the love of God."

TITLE:

The Barley Field on Fire

TEXT:

2 Samuel 14:29–31

SUMMARY:

Unlike with Absalom, when God sends for the believer and we do not respond, it is right and good for God to set fire to our barley fields, all so that we might come to Him. In our trouble, though, we are not abandoned. The Lord may frequently use loss or trial to have us come to Him—as we should have when we were called. It is best that all of us, when called, go. And when He sets ablaze our fields, that we cling evermore tightly to Him in repentance and grace.

NOTABLE QUOTES:

"Losses, too, are frequently the means God uses to fetch home His wandering sheep. Like fierce dogs they worry the wanderers back to the shepherd."

". . . your trials work your lasting good by bringing you nearer and nearer to your God."

5

The Barley
Field on Fire

*Therefore Absalom sent for Joab, to send him to
the king, but he would not come to him. And when
he sent again the second time, he would not come.
So he said to his servants, 'See, Joab's field is near
mine, and he has barley there; go and set it on fire.'
And Absalom's servants set the field on fire.*

*Then Joab arose and came to Absalom's house,
and said to him, "Why have your servants
set my field on fire?"*

2 SAMUEL 14:29-31

YOU REMEMBER THE HISTORICAL NARRATIVE. Absalom had fled from Jerusalem under fear of David's anger; he was after a time permitted to return, but he was not admitted into the presence of the king. Earnestly desiring to be restored to his former posts of honor and favor, he besought Joab to come to him, intending to request him to act as mediator. Joab, having lost much of his liking for the young prince, refused to come,

93

and though he was sent for repeatedly, he declined to attend at his desire. Absalom therefore thought of a most wicked but most effective plan of bringing Joab into his company. He bade his servants set Joab's field of barley on fire. This brought Joab down in high wrath to ask the question, "Why have your servants set my field on fire?" This was all that Absalom wanted; he wished an interview, and he was not scrupulous as to the method by which he obtained it. The burning of the barley field brought Joab into his presence, and Absalom's ends were accomplished.

Omitting the sin of the deed, we have here a picture of what is often done by our gracious God with the wisest and best design. Often He sends for us, not for His profit but for ours; He would have us come near to Him and receive a blessing at His hands, but we are foolish, coldhearted, and wicked, and we will not come. He, knowing that we will not come by any other means, sends a serious trial—He sets our barley field on fire, which He has a right to do, seeing our barley fields are far more His than they are ours.

In Absalom's case it was wrong; in God's case He has a right to do as He wills with His own. He takes away from us our most choice delight, upon which we have set our heart, and then we enquire at His hands, "Why do You contend with me? Why am I thus smitten with Your rod? What have I done to provoke You to anger?" And thus we are brought into the presence of God, and we receive blessings of infinitely more value than those temporary mercies which the Lord had taken from us. You will see, then, how I intend to use my text this morning.

As the pastor of so large a church as this, I am constantly brought into contact with all sorts of human sorrow. Frequently it is poverty—poverty which is not brought on by idleness or vice—but real poverty, and most distressing and afflicting poverty, too, because it visits those who have fought well the battle of life and have struggled hard for years and yet in their old age scarce know where bread shall come from, except that they rest upon the promise—"Your bread shall be given you, and your water shall be sure."

Messengers come to me sometimes as fast as they came to Job, bearing sad tidings concerning one and another of you. And when I have sympathized with a company of sad complaints, another set of messengers will be waiting at the door. How few families are long without severe trials; hardly a person escapes for any long season without tribulation. With impartial hand, sorrow knocks at the door of the palace and the cottage. Why all this? The Lord, we know, "does not afflict willingly, nor grieve the children of men" for naught; why can it be that He employs so many frowning servants and sends out so often His usher of the black rod? Why can it be? Perhaps I may be able to give the fitting answer to this very proper enquiry.

FOR BELIEVERS IN CHRIST

My beloved brethren and sisters in Jesus Christ, we cannot expect to avoid tribulation. If other men's barley fields are not burned, ours will be. If the Father uses the rod nowhere else, He will surely make His true children smart. Your Savior has left you a double legacy: "In the world you will have tribulation, but in Me you will have peace." You enjoy peace; you must not expect that you shall escape without the privilege of the tribulation. All wheat must be threshed, and God's threshing floor witnesses to the weight of the flail as much as any other.

But you, beloved, have four very special comforts in all your trouble. You have, first, this sweet reflection: that there is no curse in your cross. Christ was made a curse for us, and we call His cross the accursed tree, but truly since Jesus hung upon it, it is most blessed. I may now say concerning the cross of affliction, "Blessed is every man who hangs on this tree." The cross may be very heavy, especially while it is green, and our shoulders unused to carrying it; but remember, though there may be a ton-weight of sorrow in it, there is not a single ounce of the curse in it. God never punishes His children in the sense of avenging justice; He chastens as a father does his child, but He never punishes His redeemed as a judge does a criminal. How shall the Lord punish twice for one offense? If Christ took my sins and stood as my substitute, then there is no wrath of God for me. I may have to smart, but it will never be beneath the lictor's rods of justice but under the parent's rod of wisdom. O Christian, how sweet this ought to be to you!

The wrath of God is the thunderbolt which scathes the soul; and now that you are delivered from that tremendous peril, you must not be overwhelmed with the few showers and gales which Providence sends you. A God of love inflicts our sorrows; He is as good when He chastens as when He caresses. There is no more wrath in His afflicting providences than in His deeds of bounty. God may seem unkind to unbelief, but faith can always see love in His heart. Oh! what a mercy that Sinai has ceased to thunder!

You have, secondly, another ground of comfort, namely, that your troubles are all apportioned to you by divine wisdom and love. As for their number, if He appoint them ten, they never can be eleven. As for their weight, He who weighs the mountains in scales and the hills in a balance takes care to measure your troubles, and you shall not have a grain more than His infinite wisdom sees fit. The devil may seem to be turned loose upon you, but remember he is always a chained enemy. There is a tether to every trouble, and beyond that tether it can never stray. Nebuchadnezzar may heat the furnace seven times hotter than usual, but God's thermometer measures the exact degree of heat, and beyond it the flame cannot rage. Consider everything that you have to suffer as the appointment of wisdom, ruled by love, and you will rejoice in all your tribulation, knowing that it shall reveal to you the lovingkindness and wisdom of your God.

You have a third consolation, namely, that under your cross you have many special comforts. There are cordials which God gives to sick saints which He never puts to the lips of those who are in health. There is no hearing the nightingale without night, and there are some promises which only sing to us in trouble. It is in the cellar of affliction that the good old wine of the kingdom is stored. You shall never see Christ's face so well as when all others turn their backs upon you.

They sleep daintily who have Jesus to make their beds. Suffering saints are generally the most flourishing saints, and well they may be, for they are Jesus' special care. If you would find a man whose lips drop with pearls, look for one who has been in the deep waters. We seldom learn much except as it is beaten into us by the rod in Christ's schoolhouse under Madam Trouble. God's vines owe more to the pruning knife than to any other tool in the garden; superfluous shoots are sad spoilers of the vines. But even while we carry it, the cross brings present comfort; it is a dear, dear cross, all hung with roses and dripping with sweet-smelling myrrh. Humble souls count it a high honor to be thought worthy to suffer for Christ's sake. If ever heaven be opened at all to the gaze of mortals, the vision is granted to those who dwell in the Patmos of want and trouble. Furnace joys glow quite as warmly as furnace flames. Sweet are the uses of adversity and sweet are its accompaniments when the Lord is with His people.

But then, and this is the point to which my text brings me, you have this comfort, that your trials work for your lasting good by bringing you nearer and nearer to your God. My dear friends in Christ Jesus, our heavenly Father often sends for us and we will not come.

He sends for us to exercise a simpler faith in Him. We have believed, and by faith we have passed from death unto life, but our faith sometimes staggers. We have faith to lay hold upon little promises, but we are ofttimes afraid to open our mouths wide, though God has promised to fill them. He therefore sends to us. "Come, my child," says He, "come and trust Me. The veil is rent; enter into My presence and approach boldly to the throne of My grace. I am worthy of your fullest confidence; cast your cares on Me. Shake yourself from the dust of your cares, and put on your beautiful garment of faith." But, alas! though called with tones of love to the blessed exercise of this comforting grace, we will not come.

At another time He calls us to closer communion with Himself. We have been sitting on the doorstep of God's house, and He bids us advance into the banqueting hall and sup with Him, but we decline the honor. He has admitted us into the inner chambers, but there are secret rooms not yet opened to us; He invites us to enter them, but we hold back. Jesus longs to have near communion with His people. It must be a joy to a Christian to be with Christ, but it is also a joy to Jesus to be with His people, for it is written, "His delights were with the sons of men" [Prov. 8:31]. Now, one would think that if Christ did but beckon with His finger and say to us, "Draw nigh, and commune with Me," we should fly, as though we had wings to our feet. But instead we are cleaving to the dust— we have too much business, too many burdensome cares, and we forget to come, though it is our Beloved's voice which calls us to Himself.

Frequently the call is to more fervent prayer. Do you not feel in yourself, at certain seasons, an earnest longing for private prayer? And yet maybe you have quenched the Spirit in that respect and still have continued without nearness of access to God. Every day the Lord bids His people come to Him and ask what they will, and it shall be done. He is a bounteous God who sits upon the mercy seat, and He delights to give to His people the largest desires of their hearts. And yet, shame upon us, we live without exercising this power of prayer, and we miss the plenitude of blessing which would come out of that cornucopia of grace. Ah, brethren! we are verily guilty here, most of us. The Master sends to us to pray, and we will not come.

Often too He calls us to a higher state of piety. I am persuaded there are Christians as much in grace beyond ordinary Christians as ordinary Christians are beyond the profane. There are heights which common eyes have never seen, much less scaled. Would that we had grace to cleave the clouds and mount into the pure blue sky of fellowship with Christ!

We do not serve God as we should. We are cold as ice when we should be like molten metal burning our way through all opposition. We are like the barren Sahara when we should be blooming like the garden of the Lord. We give to God pence when He deserves pounds, nay, deserves our heart's blood to be coined in the service of His church and of His truth. Oh! we are but poor lovers of our sweet Lord Jesus, not fit to be His servants, much less to be His brides. O, brethren, God often calls us to higher degrees of piety, and yet we will not come.

Now, why do we permit our Lord to send for us so often without going to Him? Let your own heart give the reason in a humble confession of your offenses. We never thought we should have been so bad as we are. If an angel had told us that we should be so indifferent towards Christ, we should have said, as Hazael did to Elisha, "Is your servant a dog, that he should do this great thing?" If any of us could have seen our own history written out by a prophet's pen, we should have said, "No, it cannot be; if Christ forgives me I must love Him." And yet, hitherto, here we have been ungrateful, unbelieving, and even refusing to listen to His call or come at His bidding. Because we will not listen to the gentle call of God, there comes trouble, just as there came the burning of the barley field of Joab. Trouble comes in all sorts of shapes. Little does it matter what form it comes in, if it but makes us obey the divine calling.

Some Christians have their trial in the shape of sickness: they drag about with them a diseased body all their lives, or they are suddenly cast upon the bed of sickness. This is God's medicine, and when God's children have it, let them not think it is sent to kill them but to heal them. Much medicine the physician gives makes the man ill for a time; a clever physician knows that this is the consequence of the medicine, and thus he is not at all alarmed by the pain of his patient but expects that all this will work for good and hunt out, as it were, the original disease.

When the Lord sends us sore sickness, it for a time perhaps makes our former spiritual infirmities grow worse, for sickness often provokes impatience and murmuring against God, but in due time our proud spirits will be broken, and we shall cry for mercy. The diamond has much cutting, but its value is increased thereby, and so with the believer under the visitations of God. My brother, if you will not come to God without it, He will send you a sick bed that you may be carried on it to Him. If you will not come running, He will make you come limping. But come you must, and if by no other means, sickness shall be the black chariot in which you shall ride.

Losses, too, are frequently the means God uses to fetch home His wandering sheep. Like fierce dogs they worry the wanderers back to the shepherd. When rich and increased in goods, many professors carry their heads much too loftily and speak much too boastfully. When the Christian grows wealthy, is in good repute, has good health, and a happy family, he too often admits Mr. Carnal Security to feast at his table. If he be a true child of God, there is a rod preparing for him. Wait awhile, and it may be you will see his substance melt away as a dream. Now as these embarrassments come in one after another, he begins to be distressed about them, and betakes himself to his God. Oh! blessed waves, that wash the man on the rock of salvation! Oh! blessed cords, though they may cut the flesh if they draw us to Jesus. Losses in business are often sanctified to our soul's enriching. If you will not come to the Lord full-handed, you shall come empty. If God, in His grace, finds no other means of making you to honor Him among men, He will bring you down to the valley of poverty.

Bereavements, too—ah! What sharp cuts of the rods we get with these, my brethren! We know how the Lord sanctifies these to the bringing of His people near to Himself. Christ Himself once suffered bereavements as we have done. Bereavements might be looked upon as very sad things, but when we recollect that Jesus wept over His friend Lazarus, henceforth they are choice jewels and special favors from God. Many a mother has been stirred up to a holier life by the death of her infant. Many a husband has been led to give his heart more to Christ by the death of his wife. Do not departed spirits, like angels, beckon us up to heaven? Yes, we must look upon our new-made graves in this light and pray the Lord to dig our hearts with the funeral spade and bury our sins as we bury our departed ones.

Trials in your family, in your children, are another form of the burning barley field. I do not know, brethren, but I think a living cross is much heavier to carry than a dead one. I know some among you who have not lost your children; I could have wished you had, for they have lived to be your grief and sorrow. Ah! young man, better that your mother should have seen you perish in the birth than that you should live to disgrace your father's name. Ah! man, it were better for you that the procession had gone winding through the streets, bearing your corpse down to the grave, than that you should live to blaspheme your mother's God and laugh at the Book which is her treasure. It were better for you that you had never been born, and better for your parents too. Ah! but dear friends, even these are meant to draw us nearer to Christ.

We must not make idols of our children, and we dare not do it, when we see how manifestly God shows us that, like ourselves, they are by nature children of wrath. Sharper than an adder's tooth is an unthankful child, but the venom is turned to medicine in God's hand. You must look upon these family trials as invitations from God—sweet compulsion to make you seek His face.

Many are afflicted in another way, which is perhaps as bad as anything else—by a deep depression of spirit. They are always melancholy; they know not why. There are no stars in the night for them, and the sun gives no light by day; melancholy has marked them for her own. But even this, I think, is often the means of keeping some of them nearer to God than they would be. Too many sweets make children sick, and bitters are a good tonic. A veil is needed for some delicate complexions, lest the sun look too fiercely on them; it may be these mourners need the veil of sorrow. It is good that they have been afflicted, even with this heavy depression of spirit, because it keeps them near their God.

Then there is that other affliction, the hiding of God's countenance—how hard to bear, but how beneficial! If we will not keep near to our Lord, He is sure to hide His face. You have seen a mother walking out with her little child, when it has just learned to walk, and as she goes through the street, the little one is for running sometimes to the right, and sometimes to the left, and so the mother hides herself a moment. Then the child looks round for the mother and begins to cry, and then out comes the mother. What is the effect? Why, it will not run away from mother anymore; it is sure to keep hold of her hand afterwards. So, when we get wandering from God, He hides His face, and then, since we have a love for Him, we begin crying after Him; and when He shows His face once more, we cling to Him the more lovingly ever afterwards. So the Lord is pleased to bless our troubles to us.

Now, Christian, what about all this? Why, just this. Are you under any sharp trouble now? Then I pray you go to God as Joab went to Absalom. Make this a special season of humbling and heart-searching. Now let every besetting sin be driven out. When God sweeps, do you search? When you are under the rod, it is yours to make a full confession of past offenses and pray to be delivered from their power in the future. Or have you no trial today, my brother? Then see if there be not something which may provoke God to send one and begin now to purge yourself from all filthiness of the flesh and of the spirit by the Holy Ghost. Prevention is better than a cure, and sometimes a timely heart-searching may save us many a heart-smarting. Let us see to that then.

Or have we been afflicted, and is the affliction over now? Then, let us bless God for all that He has done, saying, "It is good for me that I have been afflicted." Let us join together in one common hymn of praise for all the lovingkindness which God has been pleased to show us in the sharp cuts of His rod. God has burned your barley field, dear friends; now go to Him, and the closer you can approach to Him, and the more firmly you can cling to Him, the better for your soul's health and comfort all your life. At the last, you and I shall sing to the praise of our afflicting God.

FOR SINNERS

God also has sent for you, O unconverted man. God has often sent for you. Early in your childhood your mother's prayers sought to woo you to a Savior's love, and your godly father's first instructions were as so many meshes of the net in which it was desired that you should be taken. But you have broken through all these and lived to sin away early impressions and youthful promises. Since then you have often been called under the ministry. Our sermons have not been all shots wide of the mark, but sometimes a hot shot has burnt its way into your conscience and you have been made to tremble. But alas! the trembling soon gave way before your old sins. Hitherto you have been called, but you refused.

You have had calls too from your Bible, from religious

books, from Christian friends. Holy zeal is not altogether dead, and it shows itself by looking after your welfare. Young man, your shopmate has sometimes spoken to you; young woman, your companion has wept over you. But still all the agency that has been employed has been up to this moment without effect; you are a stranger to the God who made you and an enemy to Christ the Savior.

Well, if these gentle means will not do, God will employ other agencies. Perhaps He has tried them already. If not, if He intends in the divine decree your eternal salvation, He will, as sure as you are a living man, use stronger ways with you. If a word will not do, He will come with a blow, though He loves to try the power of the word first. You too, my hearer, unconverted and unsaved, have had your trials. You weep as well as Christians. You may not weep for sin, but sin shall make you weep. You may abhor repentance because of its sorrow, but you shall not escape sorrow, even if you escape repentance.

You have had your sickness. Do you remember those weary days when you tossed from side to side and did but shift the place and keep the pain? Man, can you recollect your vows, which you have lived to break, and your promises with which you lied unto the eternal God? Then the Sabbath would be your delight, you said, if you were spared, and the house of God and the people of God should be dear to you and you would seek His face? But you have not done so; you have broken your covenant and have despised your promise made to God.

Or have you had losses in business? You began life well and hopefully, but nothing has prospered with you. I am not sorry for it, for I remember it is the wicked who spreads himself like a green bay tree, and it is concerning the reprobate that it is written, "There are no pangs in their death, but their strength is firm. They are not in trouble as other men, nor are they plagued like other men" [Ps. 73:4–5]. I am glad that you were plagued. I would sooner see you whipped to heaven than coached to hell.

You have had losses. What are these but God's rough messengers to tell you that there is nothing beneath the sky worth living for, to wean you from the breasts of earth and cause you to look for something more substantial than worldly riches can afford you? And you, too, have lost friends; may I recall those graves whose turf is yet so newly laid? I would not wish to make your wounds bleed afresh, but it is for your good that I bid you hearken to their solemn voice, for they say to you, "Come to your God! Be reconciled to Him!" I do not think you ever will come to Jesus unless the Holy Spirit shall employ trials to bring you. The prodigal never came back till he was hungry. I only hope that these troubles may be blessed to you.

Besides this, you have had your depression of spirit—if I mistake not, I address some who are under such depressions now. You do not know how it is, but nothing is pleasant to you. You went to the theater last night; you wished you had not. It gave you no joy, and yet you have been as merry there as any in former times. You go among your companions, and a day's pleasuring has become to you a very painful waste of time. You have lost the zest of life, and I am not sorry for it if it should make you look for a better life and trust in a world to come.

My friends, again I say, this is the burning of your barley fields. God has sent for you, and you would not come, and now He has sent messengers who are not so easily refused.

Well now, what then? If God is sending these, are you listening to them? There are some of you of whom I almost despair. God can save you, but I cannot tell how He will do it. Certainly the Word does not seem likely to be blessed. You have been called and entreated; early and late we have entreated you. Our hearts have yearned with tenderness for you, but hitherto in vain. God knows I have been hammering away at the granite, and it has not yielded yet. I have smitten the flint, and it is not broken. As for trouble, I do not see that that is likely to do you any good, for if you are smitten again, you will revolt more and more. The whole head is sick already, and the whole heart is faint. You have been beaten until from the crown of the head to the sole of your foot there is nothing but wounds, bruises, and putrefying sores. You are poor—perhaps your drunkenness has made you so. You have lost your wife—perhaps your cruelty helped to kill her. You have lost your children, and you are left a penniless, friendless, helpless beggar, and yet you will not turn to God! What now is to be done unto you? O Ephraim, what shall I do to you? Shall I give you up? How can I give you up? The heart of mercy still yearns after you. Return! Return! God help you to return, even now!

Others of you have not suffered all this in the past but are just now enduring a part of it. Let me entreat you by the mercies of God and by the blood of our Lord Jesus Christ that you despise not Him who speaks to you. God does not continue to send His messengers forever. After He has labored with you for a time, He will leave you to cursing. Behold, the King runs up the white flag of comfort today, and He invites you to come unto Him. Tomorrow He may run up the red flag of threatening, and if that answers not, He will run up the black flag of execution, and then there will be no hope. Beware! The black flag is not run up yet; the red flag is there now in trials and troubles, which are God's threatenings to you, bidding you open wide your heart that grace may enter. But if the red flag fail, the black flag must come. Perhaps it has come! God help you with broken heart to cry unto Him that you may be saved before the candle is blown out and the sun is set and the night of the dead is come on without the hope of another sun rising on a blessed resurrection.

What is the drift of all this? If now a word of mine could make you come to the King this morning—I know it will not unless God the Holy Spirit compels you to do so by His irresistible power—but if He would bless it, I would rejoice as one who finds great spoil. Why do you stand out against God? If the Lord intends your eternal salvation, your resistance will be in vain, and how will you vex yourself in after years to think that you should have stood out so long!

Why do you resist? God's battering ram is too mighty for the walls of your prejudice; He will make them fall yet. Why do you stand out against your God, against Him who loves you, who has loved you with an everlasting love and redeemed you by the blood of Christ? Why stand you out against Him who intends to lead your captivity captive and to make you yet

His rejoicing child? O that the Spirit of God would enable you, sinner, to come just as you are and put your trust in Christ. If you do so, then it is certain that your name is written in the Lamb's Book of Life, that you were chosen of God and are precious to Him, and that your head is one on which the crown of immortality is to glitter forever.

O that you would trust Christ! The joy and peace it works in the present is worth worlds, but oh! the glory, the overwhelming glory which in worlds to come shall belong to those that trust in Jesus! His blood can cleanse; His righteousness can cover; His beauty can adorn; His prayer can preserve; His advent shall glorify; His heaven shall make you blessed. Trust Him! God help you to trust Him, and He shall have all the praise, both now and forever. Amen and amen.

TITLE:
The Greatest Trial on Record

TEXT:
Psalm 2:2

SUMMARY:
The greatest and most horrific trial known to man is the trial of the Lord Jesus Christ. Throughout the entirety of His trial the Lord Jesus seeks only to accomplish the will of the Father while suffering at the hands of sinners. He displays complete patience and ultimate self-control. It is in the court of sinners that Christ displays His proof that He is the omnipotent God. Even under the hands of Pilate He displays perfect submission and self-control. Therefore, we can throw ourselves fully upon Him.

NOTABLE QUOTES:
"Trust Him; throw yourself on Him. As a man commits himself to the waters, so do you; sink or swim!"

"Either you must this day accept Christ as your King, or else His blood will be on you."

6

The Greatest Trial on Record

The kings of the earth set themselves,
and the rulers take counsel together,
*against the L*ORD*, and against His Anointed.*

PSALM 2:2

AFTER OUR LORD HAD BEEN BETRAYED by the false-hearted Judas, He was bound by the officers who had come to take Him. No doubt the cords were drawn as tight and twisted as mercilessly as possible. If we believe the traditions of the fathers, these cords cut through the flesh even to the very bones, so that all the way from the garden to the house of Annas His blood left a crimson trail. Our Redeemer was hurried along the road which crosses the brook Kedron. A second time He was made like unto David, who passed over that brook, weeping as he went; and perhaps it was on this occasion that He drank of that foul brook by the way. The brook Kedron, you know, was that into which all the filth of the sacrifices of the temple was cast, and Christ, as though He were a foul and filthy thing, must be led to the black stream.

He was led into Jerusalem by the sheep gate, the gate through which the lambs of the Passover and the sheep for sacrifice were always driven. Little did they understand that in so doing they were again following out to the very letter the significant types which God had ordained in the law of Moses. They led, I say, this Lamb of God through the sheep gate, and they hastened Him on to the house of Annas, the ex-high priest who stood high in the opinion of the rulers. Here they made a temporary call to gratify the bloodthirsty Annas with the sight of His victim. Then, hastening on, they brought Him to the house of Caiaphas, where, though it was but a little past the dead of night, many members of the Sanhedrin were assembled. In a very short time, no doubt informed by some speedy messenger, all the rest of the elders came together and sat down with great delight to the malicious work.

Let us follow our Lord Jesus Christ, not like Peter, afar off, but like John. Let us go in with Jesus into the high priest's house, and when we have tarried awhile there and have seen our Savior despitefully used, let us traverse the streets with Him till we come to the hall of Pilate, and then to the palace of Herod, and then afterwards to the place called "the pavement," where Christ is subjected to an ignominious competition with Barabbas, the murderer, and where we hear the howling of the people, "Crucify Him! Crucify Him!"

Brethren, as the Lord gave commandment concerning even the ashes and offal of the sacrifices, we ought to think no matter trivial which stands in connection with our great burnt offering. My admonition is, "Gather up the fragments that remain, so that nothing is lost." As goldsmiths sweep their shops, to save even the filings of the gold, so every word of Jesus should be treasured up as very precious. But, indeed, the narrative to which I invite you is not unimportant. Things which were purposed of old, prophesied by seers, witnessed by apostles, written by evangelists, and published by the ambassadors of God are not matters of secondary interest but deserve our solemn and devout attention. Let all our hearts be awed as we follow the King of kings in His pathway of shame and suffering.

THE HALL OF CAIAPHAS

Come we, then, to the hall of Caiaphas. After the mob had dragged our Lord from the house of Annas, they reached the palace of Caiaphas, and there a brief interval occurred before the high priest came forth to question the prisoner. How were those sad minutes spent? Was the poor victim allowed a little pause to collect His thoughts, that He might face His accusers calmly? Far from it; Luke shall tell the pitiful story: "Now the men who held Jesus mocked Him and beat Him. And having blindfolded Him, they struck Him on the face and asked Him, saying, 'Prophesy! Who is the one who struck You?'"

The officers were pausing until the chairman of the court should please to have an interview with the prisoner, and instead of suffering the accused to take a little rest before a trial so important, they spend all the time in venting their bitter malice upon

Him. Observe how they insult His claim to the Messiahship! They bind His eyes, and then, smiting Him one after another, they bid Him exercise His prophetic gift for their amusement and prophesy who it was that smote Him. Oh, shameful question! How gracious was the silence, for an answer might have withered them forever.

The day shall come when all that smite Christ shall find that He has seen them, though they thought His eyes were blinded. The day shall come, blasphemer, worldling, careless man, when everything that you have done against Christ's cause and Christ's people shall be published before the eyes of men and angels, and Christ shall answer your question—shall tell you who it is that smote Him. I speak to some this morning who have forgotten that Christ sees them, and they have ill-treated His people. I tell you, the Judge of men shall before long point you out and make you, to your shame, confess that you smote the Savior when you smote His church.

This preliminary mockery being over, Caiaphas the high priest came in. He began at once to interrogate the Lord before the public trial, doubtless with the view of catching Him in His speech. The high priest asked Him first of His disciples. We do not know what questions he asked. Our Lord Jesus on this point said not a syllable. Why this silence? Because it is not for our Advocate to accuse His disciples. He might have answered, "The cowards forsook me; when one proved a traitor, the rest took to their heels. There is one yonder, sitting by the fire, warming his hands, the same who just now denied me with an oath." But no, He would not utter a word of accusation. He whose lips are mighty to intercede for His people will never speak against them. Let Satan slander, but Christ pleads.

The high priest next asked Him concerning His doctrine, whether what He taught was not in contradiction to the original teachings of their great lawgiver Moses, and whether He had not railed at the Pharisees, reviled the scribes, and exposed the rulers. The Master gave a noble answer. Truth is never shamefaced; He boldly points to His public life as His best answer. "I spoke openly to the world. I always taught in synagogues and in the temple, where the Jews always meet, and in secret I have said nothing. Why do you ask Me? Ask those who have heard Me what I said to them. Indeed they know what I said." No sophistries—no attempt at evasion; the best armor for truth is her own naked breast. He had preached in the marketplaces, on the mountain's brow, and in the temple courts; nothing had been done in a corner.

Happy is the man who can make so noble a defense. Where can the arrow pierce the man arrayed in so complete a panoply? Little did that arch-knave Caiaphas gain by his crafty questioning. For the rest of the questioning, our Lord Jesus said not a word in self-defense. He knew that it availed not for a lamb to plead with wolves. He was well aware that whatever He said would be misconstrued and made a fresh source of accusation, and He willed, moreover, to fulfill the prophecy, "He was led as a lamb to the slaughter, and as a sheep before her shearers is silent, so He opened not His mouth." But what power He exerted in thus remaining silent!

Perhaps nothing displays more fully the omnipotence of

Christ than this power of self-control. Control the Deity? What power less than divine can attempt the task? Behold, my brethren, the Son of God does more than rule the winds and commend the waves; He restrains Himself. And when a word, a whisper, would have refuted His foes and swept them to their eternal destruction, He "opened not His mouth." He who opened His mouth for His enemies will not utter a word for Himself. If ever silence were more than golden, it is this deep silence under infinite provocation.

During this preliminary examination, our Lord suffered an outrage which needs a passing notice. When He had said, "Ask those who have heard Me," some over-officious person in the crowd struck Him in the face. Now, considering that our blessed Lord suffered so much, this one might seem unimportant, only it happens to be the subject of prophecy in the book of Micah 5:1, "They will strike the judge of Israel with a rod on the cheek." This smiting while under trial is peculiarly atrocious. To strike a man while he is pleading in his own defense would surely be a violation of the laws even of barbarians. It brought Paul's blood into his face and made him lose his balance when the high priest ordered them to smite him on the mouth. I think I hear his words of burning indignation: "God will strike you, you white-washed wall! For you sit to judge me according to the law, and do you command me to be struck contrary to the law?" [Acts 23:3]. How soon the servant loses his temper; how far more glorious the meekness of the Master. What a contrast do these gentle words afford us—"If I have spoken evil, bear witness of the evil; but if well, why do you strike Me?" [John 18:23].

But now the court is all sitting; the members of the great Sanhedrin are all in their various places, and Christ is brought forth for the public trial before the highest ecclesiastical court, though it is a foregone conclusion that by hook or by crook they will find Him guilty. They scour the neighborhood for witnesses. There were fellows to be found in Jerusalem who were ready to be bought on either side and, provided they were well paid, would swear to anything. But for all this, though the witnesses were ready to perjure themselves, they could not agree one with another; being heard separately, their tales did not tally. At last two came, with some degree of similarity in their witness; they were both liars, but for once the two liars had struck the same note.

They declared that He said, "I will destroy this temple made with hands, and within three days I will build another made without hands." Now here was, first, misquotation. He never said, "I will destroy the temple." His words were, "Destroy this temple, and in three days I will raise it up." See how they add to His words and twist them to their own ends. Then again, they not only misquoted the words, but they misrepresented the sense, because He spoke concerning the temple of His body and not the literal temple in which they worshiped. This they must have known. He said, "Destroy this temple," and the accompanying action might have showed them that He meant His own body, which was raised by His glorious resurrection after destruction upon the cross.

Let us add that even when thus misrepresented, the witness was not sufficient as the foundation of a capital charge. Surely there could be nothing worthy of death in a man's saying, "Destroy this temple, and I will build it in three days." But where men have made up their minds to hate Christ, they will hate Him without a cause. You that are adversaries of Christ—and there are some such here today—I know you try to invent some excuse for your opposition to His holy religion, but you know that your witness is not true, and your trial in conscience through which you pass the Savior is but a mock one. Submit yourselves to Him now.

Finding that their witness, even when tortured to the highest degree, was not strong enough, the high priest, to get [some] matter of accusation, adjured Him by the Most High God to answer whether He was the Christ, "the Son of the Blessed." Being thus adjured, our Master would not set us an example of cowardice. He said, "I am," and then, to show how fully He knew this to be true, He added, "you will see the Son of Man sitting at the right hand of the Power, and coming with the clouds of heaven." I cannot understand what Unitarians do with this incident. Christ was put to death on a charge of blasphemy for having declared Himself to be the Son of God. Was not that the time when any sensible person would have denied the accusation? If He had not really claimed to be the Son of God, would He not now have spoken? But no, He seals it with His blood; He bears open testimony before the herd of His accusers.

Now the thing is done. They want no further evidence. The judge, forgetting the impartiality which becomes his station, pretends to be wonderfully struck with horror, rends his garments, turns round to ask his co-assessors whether they need any further witness, and they, all too ready, hold up their hands in token of unanimity, and He is at once condemned to die. Ah! brethren, and no sooner condemned than the high priest, stepping down from his divan, spits in His face, and then the Sanhedrin follow and smite Him on His cheek. Then they turn Him down to the rabble that had gathered in the court, and they buffet Him from one to the other and spit upon His blessed cheeks and smite Him. They blindfold Him for a second time, place Him in the chair, and as they smite Him with their fists they cry, "Prophet! Prophet! Prophet! Who is it that smote You? Prophesy unto us!" And thus the Savior passed a second time through that most brutal and ignominious treatment. If we had tears, if we had sympathies, if we had hearts, we should prepare to shed those tears, to awake those sympathies, and break those hearts now. O You, Lord of life and glory! How shamefully were You treated by those who pretended to be the curators of holy truth, the conservators of integrity, and the teachers of the law!

Having thus sketched the trial as briefly as I could, let me just say, that, throughout the whole of this trial before the ecclesiastical tribunal, it is manifest that they did all they could to pour contempt upon His two claims—to Deity and to Messiahship. Now, this morning you and I must range ourselves on one of two sides. Either this day we must cheerfully acknowledge His Godhead and accept Him also as the Messiah, the Savior promised of old to us, or else we must take our post with the adversaries of God and of His Christ. Will you ask yourself the question: on which side will you now stand?

I pray you, do not think that Christ's Deity needs any

further proof than that which this one court gives. My dear friends, there is no religion under heaven, no false religion, which would have dared to hazard such a statement, as that yonder Man who was spit upon and buffeted was none other than incarnate God. No false religion would venture to draw upon the credulity of its followers to that extent. What! that Man there who speaks not a word, who is mocked, despised, rejected, made nothing of—what! He "very God of very God"? You do not find Mohammed, nor any false prophet, asking any person to believe a doctrine so extraordinary. They know too well that there is a limit even to human faith, and they have not ventured upon such a marvelous assertion as this, that yonder despised Man is none other than the upholder of all things. No false religion would have taught a truth so humbling to Him who is its founder and Lord. Besides, it is not in the power of any man-made religion to have conceived such a thought. That Deity should willingly submit to be spit upon to redeem those whose mouths vented the spittle! In what book do you read such a wonder as this?

We have pictures drawn from imagination; we have been enchanted along romantic pages, and we have marveled at the creative flights of human genius; but where did you ever read such a thought as this? "God was made flesh and dwelt among us"—He was despised, scourged, mocked, treated as though He were the offscouring of all things, brutally treated, worse than a dog, and all out of pure love to His enemies. Why, the thought is such a great one, so God-like, the compassion in it is so divine, that it must be true. None but God could have thought of such a thing as this stoop from the highest throne in glory to the cross of deepest shame and woe.

And do you think that if the doctrine of the cross were not true, such effects would follow from it? Would those South Sea Islands, once red with the blood of cannibalism, be now the abode of sacred song and peace? Would this island be what it is, through the influence of the benign gospel of God, if that gospel were a lie? The thing is not false. And that He is Messiah, who shall doubt? If God should send a prophet, what better prophet could you desire? What character would you seek to have exhibited more completely human and divine? What sort of a Savior would you wish for? What could better satisfy the cravings of conscience? Who could commend Himself more fully to the affections of the heart? He must be, we feel at once, as we see Him, one alone by Himself, with no competitor. He must be the Messiah of God.

Come, now, sirs, on which side will you range yourselves? Will you smite Him? "I will not," says one, "but I do not accept nor believe in Him." In that you smite Him. "I do not hate Him," says another, "but I am not saved by Him." In refusing His love you smite Him. That suffering Man stands in the room, and place, and stead of every one that will believe on Him. Trust Him! Trust Him! You have then accepted Him as your God, as your Messiah. Refuse to trust Him? You have smitten Him; and you may think it little to do this today, but when He rides upon the clouds of heaven you will see your sin in its true light, and you will shudder to think that ever you could have refused Him who now reigns "King of kings and

Lord of lords." God help you to accept Him as your God and Christ today!

IN FRONT OF THE ROMANS

The Romans had taken away from the Jews the power to put a person to death. They sometimes did it still, but they did it, as in the case of Stephen, by popular tumult. Now, in our Savior's case they could not do this because there was still a strong feeling in favor of Christ among the people, a feeling so strong that had they not been bribed by the rulers, they would never have said, "Crucify Him! Crucify Him!" You will remember that the priests and rulers did not arrest Him on the feast day, "lest" said they, "there be an uproar of the people."

Besides, the Jewish way of putting a person to death was by stoning: hence, unless there was a sufficient number of persons who hated him, a person would never get put to death at all. That is why the method of putting to death by stoning was chosen, because if a person was generally thought to be innocent, very few persons would stone him; and although he would be somewhat maimed, his life might possibly be spared. They thought the Savior might escape as He did at other times when they took up stones to stone Him. Moreover they desired to put Him to the death of the accursed; they would confound Him with slaves and criminals; therefore they hound Him away to Pilate.

The distance was about a mile. He was bound in the same cruel manner and was doubtless cut by the cords. He had already suffered most dreadfully: remember the bloody sweat of last Sabbath week. Then remember that He has already twice been beaten; and He is now hurried along, without any rest or refreshment, just as the morning is breaking. He is bound, and they hurry Him along the road. Here the Romish writers supply a great number of particulars of anguish out of their very fertile imaginations.

After they had brought Him there a difficulty occurred. These holy people, these very righteous elders, could not come into the company of Pilate, because Pilate, being a Gentile, would defile them. There was a broad space outside the palace, like a raised platform, where Pilate was wont to sit on those high days, that he might not touch these blessed Jews. So he came out on the pavement, and they themselves went not into the hall. Always notice that sinners who can swallow camels will strain at gnats, crowds of men who will do great sins are very much afraid of committing some little things which they think will affect their religion. In fact, most hypocrites run for shelter to some close observance of days, ceremonies, and observations, when they have slighted the weightier matters of the law.

Pilate receives Him bound. The charge brought against Him was not, of course, blasphemy. Pilate would have laughed at that and declined all interference. They accused Him of stirring up sedition, pretending to be a king, and teaching that it was not right to pay tribute to Caesar. This last charge was a clear and manifest lie. Did not He send to the fish's mouth to get the money? Did He not tell the Herodians—"Render therefore to Caesar the things that are Caesar's"? He stir up a sedition—the Man that had "nowhere to lay His head"? He pretend to snatch the diadem from Caesar—the Man who hid Himself when the people would have taken Him by force and made Him a king? Nothing can be more atrociously false.

Pilate examines Him and discovers at once, both from His silence and from His answer, that He is a most extraordinary person; he perceives that the kingdom He claims is something supernatural; he cannot understand it. He asks him why He came into the world; the reply puzzles and amazes him, to "bear witness to the truth," says He. Now, that was a thing no Roman understood, for a hundred years before Pilate came, Jugurtha said of the city of Rome, "a city for sale." Bribery, corruption, falsehood, treachery, villainy, these were the gods of Rome, and truth had fled the seven hills; the very meaning of the word was scarcely known.

So Pilate turned on his heel, and said, "What is truth?" As much as to say, "I am the procurator of this part of the country; all I care for is money." "What's truth?" I do not think he asked the question, "What is truth?" as if he seriously desired to know what it really was, for surely he would have paused for the divine reply and not have gone away from Christ the moment afterwards. He said, "Pshaw; what's truth?" Yet there was something so awful about the prisoner that his wife's dream, and her message, all worked upon the superstitious fears of this very weak-minded ruler. So he went back and told the Jews a second time, "I find no fault in him." When they said, "He stirs up the people, teaching throughout all Judea, beginning from Galilee to this place," he caught at that word "Galilee." "Now," he thought, "I will be rid of this man; the people shall have their way, and yet I will not be guilty." "Galilee?" said he; "why, Herod is ruler there; you had better take Him to Herod at once." He thus gained two or three points. He made Herod his friend, and he hoped to exonerate himself of his crime and yet please the mob. Away they go to Herod.

Oh! I think I see that blessed Lamb of God again hounded through the streets. Did you ever read such a tale? No martyr was ever harried thus as the Savior was. We must not think that His agonies were all confined to the cross; they were endured in those streets—in those innumerable blows, kicks, strikings with the fist that He had to bear.

They took Him before Herod, and Herod, having heard of His miracles, thought to see some wonderful thing, some piece of jugglery, done in his presence. And when Christ refused to speak and would not plead before "that fox" at all, then Herod treated Him with a sneer. They made nothing of Him. Can you picture the scene? Herod, his captains, his lieutenants, all down to the meanest soldiers, treat the Savior with a broad grin! Look at His cheeks, all bruised where they have been smiting Him: is that the color of royalty's complexion? "Look," say they, "He is emaciated, He is covered with blood, as though He had been sweating drops of blood all night. Is that the imperial purple?" And so they "made nothing of him" and despised His kingship. And Herod said, "Bring out that costly white robe; you know, if He be a king, let us dress Him so," and so the white robe is put on Him—not a purple one that Pilate put on afterwards.

He has two robes put on Him—the one put on by the Jews, the other by the Gentiles; seeming to be a fit comment on that passage in Solomon's song where the spouse says, "My beloved is white and ruddy." White with the gorgeous robe which marked Him King of the Jews and then red with the purple robe which Pilate afterwards cast upon His shoulders, which proved Him King of nations too. And so Herod and his men of war, after treating Him as shamefully as they could, sent Him back again to Pilate. It is another journey along those streets, another scene of shameful tumult, bitter scorn, and cruel smitings. Why, He dies a hundred deaths, my brethren, it is not one—it is death on death the Savior bears as He is dragged from tribunal to tribunal.

See, they bring Him to Pilate a second time. Pilate again is anxious to save Him and says he will release Him. "No, no," they say; and they clamor greatly. He proposes a cruel alternative, which yet he meant for tender mercy. "I will therefore chastise Him and release Him." He gave Him over to his lictors to be scourged. The Roman scourge was a most dreadful instrument. It was made of the sinews of oxen and little sharp pieces of bone, which cause the most frightful lacerations. Little sharp pieces, splinters of bone, were intertwisted among the sinews, so that every time the lash came down some of these pieces of bone went right into the flesh and tore off heavy thongfuls, and not only the blood but the very flesh would be rent away. The Savior was tied to the column and thus beaten. He had been beaten before, but this of the Roman lictor was probably the most severe of His flagellations.

After Pilate had beaten Him, he gave Him up to the soldiers for a short time, that they might complete the mockery and so be able to witness that Pilate had no idea of the royalty of Jesus and no complicity in any supposed treason. The soldiers put a crown of thorns on His head, bowed before Him, spat on Him, and put a reed in His hands. They smote the crown of thorns into His temple, and they covered Him with a purple robe. Then Pilate brought Him out, saying, "Behold the man!" I believe he did it out of pity. He thought, "Now I have wounded Him and cut Him to pieces thus, I will not kill Him; that sight will move their hearts." Oh! that *Ecce Homo* ought to have melted their hearts, if Satan had not made them harder than flints and sterner than steel. But no, they cry, "Crucify Him! Crucify Him!"

So Pilate listens to them again, and they change their note, "He has spoken blasphemy." This was a wrong charge to bring, for Pilate, having his superstition again aroused, is the more afraid to put him to death, and he comes out again, and says, "I find no fault in him." What a strong contest between good and evil in that man's heart! But they cried out again, "If you let this man go, you are not Caesar's friend." They hit the mark this time, and he yields to their clamor. He brings forth a basin of water, and he washes his hands before them all, and he says, "I am innocent of the blood of this just Person. You see to it." A poor way of escaping! That water could not wash the blood from his hands, though their cry did bring the blood on their heads.

When that is done, Pilate takes the last desperate step of sitting down on the pavement in royal state; he condemns Jesus and bids them take Him away. But ere He is taken to execution, the dogs of war shall snap at Him again. The Jews, no doubt having bribed the soldiers to excessive zeal of scorn, they a second time took Him back again, and once more they mocked Him, once more they spat upon Him, and treated Him shamefully. So, you see, there was once when He first went to the house of Caiaphas; then after He was condemned there; then Herod and his men of war; then Pilate after the scourging; and then the soldiers, after the ultimate condemnation.

See you not how manifestly "He is despised and rejected by men, a Man of sorrows acquainted with grief. And we hid, as it were, our faces from Him; He was despised, and we did not esteem Him" [Isa. 53:3]. I do not know when I ever more heartily wished to be eloquent than I do now. I am talking to my own lips, and saying, "Oh! that these lips had language worthy of the occasion!" I do but faintly sketch the scene. I cannot lay on the glowing colors. Oh, that I could set forth Your grief, You Man of Sorrows! God the Holy Ghost impress it on your memories and on your souls and help you pitifully to consider the griefs of your blessed Lord.

I will now leave this point, when I have made this practical application of it. Remember, dear friends, that this day, as truly as on that early morning, a division must be made among us. Either you must this day accept Christ as your King, or else His blood will be on you. I bring my Master out before your eyes, and say to you, "Behold your King." Are you willing to yield obedience to Him? He claims first your implicit faith in His merit: will you yield to that? He claims, next, that you will take Him to be Lord of your heart and that, as He shall be Lord within, so He shall be Lord without. Which shall it be? Will you choose Him now? Does the Holy Spirit in your soul say, "Bow the knee, and take Him as your king?" Thank God, then. But if not, His blood is on you, to condemn you. You crucified Him. Pilate, Caiaphas, Herod, the Jews, and Romans all meet in you. You scourged Him; you said, "Let Him be crucified." Do not say it was not so. You join their clamors when you refuse Him. Come to the fountain of His blood, and wash and be clean.

BEFORE THE PEOPLE

Christ underwent yet a third trial. He was not only tried before the ecclesiastical and civil tribunals, but He was tried before the great democratic tribunal, that is, the assembly of the people in the street. You will say, "How?" Well, the trial was somewhat singular, but yet it was really a trial. Barabbas—a thief, a felon, a murderer, a traitor—had been captured. He was probably one of a band of murderers who were accustomed to come up to Jerusalem at the time of the feast, carrying daggers under their cloaks to stab persons in the crowd, and rob them, and then he would be gone again. Besides that, he had tried to stir up sedition, setting himself up possibly as a leader of banditti. Christ was put into competition with this villain. The two were presented before the popular eye, and to the shame of manhood, to the disgrace of Adam's race, the perfect, loving, tender, sympathizing, disinterested Savior was met with the word, "Crucify Him!" And Barabbas, the thief, was preferred. The same thing is put before you this morning—the very same thing—and every unregenerate man will make the same choice that the Jews did, and only men renewed by grace will act upon the contrary principle.

I say, friend, this day I put before you Christ Jesus or your sins. The reason why many come not to Christ is because they cannot give up their lusts, their pleasures, their profits. Sin is Barabbas; sin is a thief; it will rob your soul of its life; it will rob God of His glory. Sin is a murderer; it stabbed our father Adam; it slew our purity. Sin is a traitor; it rebels against the King of heaven and earth. If you prefer sin to Christ, Christ has stood at your tribunal, and you have given in your verdict that sin is better than Christ.

We come not to Christ because of the viciousness of our nature and depravity of our heart; and this is the depravity of your heart, that you prefer darkness to light, put bitter for sweet, and choose evil as your good. Well, I think I hear one saying, "Oh! I would be on Jesus Christ's side, but I did not look at it in that light. I thought the question was, 'Would He be on my side?' I am such a poor guilty sinner that I would fain stand anywhere, if Jesus' blood would wash me." Sinner! Sinner! If you talk like that, then I will meet you right joyously. Never was a man one with Christ till Christ was one with him.

You cannot be willing to come to Christ, and yet Christ reject you. God forbid we should suppose the possibility of any sinner crying after the Savior, and the Savior saying, "No, I will not have you." "Well," says one, "then I would have Him today. How can I do it?" There is nothing asked of you but this. Trust Him! Trust Him! Believe that God put Him in the stead of men; believe that what He suffered was accepted by God instead of their punishment; believe that this great equivalent for punishment can save you. Trust Him; throw yourself on

Him. As a man commits himself to the waters, so do you; sink or swim! You will never sink, you will never sink; for "he who hears My word and believes in Him who sent Me has everlasting life, and shall not come into judgment."

TITLE:

A Bottle in the Smoke

TEXT:

Psalm 119:83

SUMMARY:

The reality of the Christian life is that God's people will have their own trials. Whether sickness, pains, poverty, or death, trials will come forth in the smoke. The smoke is made from the flames that begin to burn what we care more deeply for than God. Whether it be comforts, jobs, or even children, the flames of trials place us within their smoke. What accompanies the smoke is the truth that Christians feel their suffering; pain is not absent from them. Yet despite all this, the law of God does not abandon them or their minds in their troubles and helps them stand fast.

NOTABLE QUOTES:

"His precepts are a light and easy yoke; but they are one which no man must cast from his shoulder. All must carry the commands of Christ, and all who hope to be saved by Him must take up his cross daily and follow Him."

"The smoke and heat soon dry every atom of moisture out of us. All our hope is gone, all our strength is departed, and then we feel that we are empty sinners, and want a full Christ to save us."

"I know—poor, weak, and helpless though I am—that I have a rich Almighty Friend. If you can stand a little smoke, then you may believe yourself to be a child of God."

7

A Bottle in the Smoke

For I am become like a bottle in the smoke;
yet do I not forget thy statutes.

PSALM 119:83 KJV

THE FIGURE OF "A BOTTLE IN THE SMOKE" is essentially oriental; we must therefore go to the East for its explanation. This we will supply to our hearers and readers in the words of the author of the *Pictorial Bible*:

> This doubtless refers to a leathern bottle, of kid or goat-skin. The peasantry of Asia keep many articles, both dry and liquid, in such bottles, which, for security, are suspended from the roof, or hung against the walls of their humble dwellings. Here they soon become quite black with smoke; for as, in the dwellings of the peasantry, there are seldom any chimneys, and the smoke can only escape

through an aperture in the roof, or by the door, the apartment is full of dense smoke whenever a fire is kindled in it. And in those nights and days, when the smokiness of the hovels in which we daily rested during a winter's journey in Persia, Armenia, and Turkey, seemed to make the cold and weariness of actual travel a relief, we had ample occasion to observe the peculiar blackness of such skin vessels, arising from the manner in which substances offering a surface of this sort receive the full influence of the smoke and detain the minute particles of soot which rest upon them. When such vessels do not contain liquids, and are not quite filled by the solids which they hold, they contract a shrunk and shrivelled appearance, to which the Psalmist may also possibly allude as well as to the blackness. But we presume that the leading idea refers to the latter circumstance, as in the East blackness has an opposite signification to the felicitous meaning of whiteness. David had doubtless seen bottles of this description hanging up in his tent when a wanderer; and though he might have had but few in his palace, yet in the cottages of his own poor people he had, no doubt, witnessed them. Hence he says of himself, "I am become," by trouble and affliction, by trial and persecution, "like a bottle in the smoke; yet do I not forget thy statutes."

First, God's people have their trials—they get put in the smoke; secondly, God's people feel their trials—they "become like a bottle in the smoke"; thirdly, God's people do not forget God's statutes in their trials—"I am become like a bottle in the smoke; yet do I not forget thy statutes."

GOD'S PEOPLE HAVE THEIR TRIALS

This is an old truth, as old as the everlasting hills, because trials were in the covenant, and certainly the covenant is as old as the eternal mountains. It was never designed by God when He chose His people that they should be an untried people, that they should be chosen to peace and safety, to perpetual happiness here below, and to freedom from sickness and the pains of mortality. But rather, on the other hand, when He made the covenant, He made the rod of the covenant too. When He drew up the charter of privileges, He also drew up the charter of chastisements. When He gave us the roll of heirship, He put down the rods amongst the things to which we should inevitably be heirs.

Trials are a part of our lot; they were predestined for us in God's solemn decrees. As surely as the stars are fashioned by His hands, so surely are our trials weighed in scales. He has predestinated their season and their place, their intensity and the effect they shall have upon us. Good men must never expect to escape troubles; if they do, they shall be disappointed; some of their predecessors have escaped them.

Mark Job, of whose patience you have heard. Read you well of Abraham, for he had his trials, and by his faith under them he became "the father of the faithful." Note well the biographies of all the patriarchs, the prophets, the apostles and martyrs, and you shall discover none of those, whom God made vessels of mercy, who were not hung up like bottles in the smoke. When born again, it does seem as if we had a birth to double trouble, and double toil and trouble come to the man who has double

SPURGEON ON PERSEVERING THROUGH TRIALS

grace and double mercy bestowed upon him. Good men must have their trials; they must expect to be like bottles in the smoke.

Sometimes these trials arise from the poverty of their condition. It is the bottle in the cottage which gets into the smoke, not the bottle in the palace. So with God's poor people; they must expect to have smoke in their dwellings. We should suppose that smoke does not enter into the house of the rich, although even then our supposition would be false. Certainly we must suppose there is more smoke where the chimney is ill built and the home is altogether of bad construction.

It is the poverty of the Arab that puts his bottle in the smoke, so the poverty of Christians exposes them to much trouble, and inasmuch as God's people are for the most part poor, for that reason must they always be for the most part in affliction. We shall not find many of God's people in the higher ranks; not many of them shall ever be illustrious in this world. Until happier times come, when kings shall be their nursing fathers and queens their nursing mothers, it must still be true that God has chosen the poor in this world, rich in faith, that they should be heirs of the kingdom. Poverty has its privileges, for Christ has lived in it; but it has its ills, its smoke, its trials. You know not sometimes how you shall be provided for. You are often pinched for food and raiment, you are vexed with anxious cares, you wonder whence tomorrow's food shall come and where you shall obtain your daily supplies. It is because of your poverty that you are hung up like a bottle in the smoke.

Many of God's people, however, are not poor; and even if they are, poverty does not occasion so much trouble to them as some suppose. For God, in the midst of poverty, makes His children very glad and so cheers their hearts in the cottage that they scarce know whether it be a palace or a hovel. Yea, He sends such sweet music across the waters of their woe that they know not whether they be on dry land or not.

But there are other trials: and this brings us to remark that our trials frequently result from our comforts. What makes the smoke? Why, it is the fire by which the Arab warms his hands that smokes his bottle, and smokes him too. So, beloved, our comforts usually furnish us with troubles. It is the law of nature that there should never be a good without having an ill connected with it. What if the stream fertilizes the land? It can sometimes drown the inhabitants. What if the fire cheers us? Does it not frequently consume our dwellings? What if the sun enlightens us? Does it not sometimes scorch and smite us with its heat? There is nothing good without its ill; there is no fire without its smoke.

The fire of our comfort will always have the smoke of trial with it. You will find it so, if you instance the comforts you have in your own family. You have relations; mark you, every relationship engenders its trial, and every fresh relationship upon which you enter opens to you, at one time certainly, a new source of joys, but infallibly also a new source of sorrows. Are you parents? Your children are your joy, but those children cause you some smoke because you fear, lest they should not be brought up in "the nurture and admonition of the Lord." And it may be, when they come to riper years, that they will grieve your spirits—God grant they may not break your hearts by their sins!

You have wealth. Well, that has its joys with it; but still, has it not its trials and its troubles? Has not the rich man more to care for than the poor? He who has nothing sleeps soundly, for the thief will not bother him; but he who has abundance often trembles lest the rough wind should blow down what he has built.

Just as the birds that visit us fly away from us, so do our joys bring sorrow with them. In fact, joy and sorrow are twins; the blood which runs in the veins of sorrow runs in the veins of joy too. For what is the blood of sorrow, is it not the tear? And what is the blood of joy? When we are full of joy, do we not weep? The same drop which expresses joy is sorrow's own emblem; we weep for joy, and we weep for sorrow.

Our fire gives smoke to tell us that our comforts have their trials with them. Christian men! You have extraordinary fires which others have never kindled; expect then to have extraordinary smoke. You have the presence of Christ, but then you will have the smoke of fear, lest you should lose it. You have the promise of God's Word—there is the fire of it—but you have the smoke sometimes when you read it without the illumination of God's Spirit. You have the joy of assurance, but you have also the smoke of doubt, which blows into your eyes and wellnigh blinds you. You have your trials, and your trials arise from your comforts. The more comfort you have, the more fire you have, the more sorrows shall you have, and the more smoke.

Again, the ministry is the great fire by which Christian men warm their hands, but the ministry hath much smoke with it. How often have you come to this house of God and had your spirits lifted up! But perhaps as often you have come here to be cast down. Your harp strings at times have been all loose; you could not play a tune of joy upon them. You have come here, and Christ tuned your harp so that it could awake "like David's harp of solemn sound." But at other times you have come here and had all the rejoicings removed from you by some solemn, searching sermon. This pulpit, which is intended at times to give you fire, is also intended to have smoke with it. It would not be God's pulpit if no smoke issued from it. When God made Sinai His pulpit, Sinai was altogether on a smoke.

I think, however, that David had one more thought. The poor bottle in the smoke keeps there for a long time, till it gets black; it is not just one puff of smoke that comes upon it. The smoke is always going up, always girding the poor bottle; it lives in an atmosphere of smoke. So, beloved, some of us hang up like bottles in the smoke for months or for a whole year. No sooner do you get out of one trouble than you tumble into another; no sooner do you get up one hill than you have to mount another; it seems to be all uphill to heaven with you. You are always in the smoke. You are linked perhaps with an ungodly partner, or perhaps you are of a singular temperament that naturally puts clouds and darkness round about you. Well, beloved, that was the condition of David. He was not just sometimes in trial, but it seemed as if trials came to him every day. Each day had its cares; each hour carried on its wings some fresh tribulation. Instead of bringing joy, each moment did but toll the knell of happiness and bring another grief. Well, if this is your case, fear not. You are not alone in your trials, but you see the truth of what is uttered here: you are like bottles in the smoke.

GOD'S PEOPLE FEEL THEIR TROUBLES

God's people are in the smoke, and they are like bottles in the smoke. There are some things that you might hang up in the smoke for many a day, and they would never be much changed because they are so black now that they could never be made any blacker, and so shriveled now that they never could become any worse. But the poor skin bottle shrivels up in the heat, gets blacker, and shows at once the effect of the smoke; it is not an unfeeling thing, like a stone, but it is at once affected.

Now, some men think that grace makes a man unable to feel suffering. I have heard people insinuate that the martyrs did not endure much pain when they were being burned to death, but this is a mistake. Christian men are not like stones; they are like bottles in the smoke. In fact, if there be any difference, a Christian man feels his trials more than another, because he traces them to God, and that makes them more acute. But at the same time it makes them more easy to bear, because he believes they will work the comfortable fruits of righteousness. A dog will bite the stone that is thrown at it, but a man would resent the man that threw the stone. Stupid, foolish, carnal unbelief quarrels with the trial; but faith goes into the court of King's bench at once, and asks its God, "Why do you contend with me?" But even faith itself does not avert the pain of chastisement; it enables us to endure but does not remove the trial. The Christian is not wrong in giving way to his feelings; did not his Master shed tears when Lazarus was dead? And did He not, when on the cross, utter the exceeding bitter cry, "My God! My God! Why have You forsaken Me?" Our Heavenly Father never intended to take away our griefs when under trial. He does not put us beyond the reach of the flood but builds us an ark, in which we float until the water be ultimately assuaged, and we rest on the Ararat of heaven forever. He gives us grace to endure our trials and to sing His praises while we suffer. I feel what God lays upon me.

The trial that we do not feel is no trial at all. We sometimes meet with persons who say, "I could bear that trial if it did not touch my feelings." Of course you could, for then it would be no trial at all. It is feeling that makes it a trial; the essence of the trial lies in my feeling it. And God intended His trials to be felt. His rods are not made of wheat straw; they are made of true birch, and His blows fall just where we feel them. He does not strike us on the iron plates of our armor, but He smites us where we are sure to be affected.

And yet more: trials which are not felt are unprofitable trials. If there be no blueness in the wound, then the soul is not made better; if there be no crying out, then there will be no emptying out of our depravity. It is just so much as we feel that we are profited, but a trial unfelt must be a trial unsanctified. A trial under which we do not feel at all cannot be a blessing to us, because we are only blessed by feeling it, under the agency of God's Holy Spirit.

Christian man! Do not blush because you are like a bottle in the smoke, because you are sensitive under affliction, for so you ought to be. Do not let others say you ought not feel it so much that your husband is dead, or your child is dead, or you have lost your property. Just tell them that you ought because God sent the trouble. That is patience: not when we do not feel but when we feel it and say, "Though He slay me, yet will I trust Him."

Now, a bottle, when it is in the smoke, gets very black. So does the Christian, when he is in the smoke of trial, or in the smoke of the gospel ministry, or the smoke of persecution, get very black to his own esteem. It is marvelous how bright we are when everything goes right with us, but it is equally marvelous how black we get when a little tribulation comes upon us. We think very well of ourselves while there is no smoke, but let the smoke come and it reveals the blackness of our hearts. Trials teach us what we are. They dig up the soil and let us see what we are made of; they are good for this reason.

A bottle that hangs up in the smoke will become very useless. So do we, often, when we are under a trying ministry or a trying providence feel that we are so very useless, good for nothing, like a bottle that has been hung up in the smoke. We feel that we are no use to anybody—that we are poor unprofitable creatures. In our joys we are honorable creatures. We scarcely think the Creator could do without us, but when we are in trouble, we feel, "I am a worm, and no man"—good for nothing; let me die.

And then a bottle in the smoke is an empty bottle. It would not have been hung up in the smoke unless it had been empty. And very often under trials how empty we become. We are full enough in our joys, but the smoke and heat soon dry every atom of moisture out of us. All our hope is gone, all our strength is departed, and then we feel that we are empty sinners and want a full Christ to save us. We are like bottles in the smoke.

Have I described any of your characters? I dare say some of you are like bottles in the smoke. You do feel your trials; you have a soft, tender heart, and the arrows of the Almighty sink fast in it. You are like a piece of seaweed, affected by every change of the weather, not like a piece of rock that might be hung up and would never change. You are capable of being affected, and it is quite right you should be: you are to "become like a bottle in the smoke."

CHRISTIANS DO NOT FORGET GOD'S STATUTES

What are God's statutes? God has two kinds of statutes, both of them engraved in eternal brass. The first are the statutes of His commands, and of these He has said, "till heaven and earth pass away, one jot or one tittle will by no means pass from the law till all is fulfilled." These statutes are like the statutes of the Medes and Persians; they are binding upon all His people. His precepts are a light and easy yoke, but they are one which no man must cast from his shoulders. All must carry the commands of Christ, and all who hope to be saved by Him must take up his cross daily and follow Him. And then again there are statutes of promise, which are equally firm, each of them as immortal as God who uttered them. David did not forget these, for he said of them, "Your statutes have been my songs in the house of my pilgrimage."

Why was it David still held fast by God's statutes? First of all, David was not a bottle in the fire, or else he would have forgotten them. Our trials are smoke, but not fire; they are very uncomfortable, but they do not consume us. In other parts of Scripture the figure of fire may be applied to our trials, but here it would not be appropriate, because the bottle would be burned up directly if it were in the fire. It is well for you,

O Christian, that there is more smoke than fire in your trials. And there is no cause why you should forget your God in your troubles. They may have a tendency to drive you from Him, but like great waves they often wash the driftwood of the poor lost barks upon the beach of God's love. And the mast that might have floated out to sea once more is made to do fresh service. So are you, Christian, washed on shore by the waves of your trouble, and never are you washed away by them: "I have not forgotten your statutes."

Another reason why David did not forget God's statutes was that Jesus Christ was in the smoke with him, and the statutes were in the smoke with him too. God's statutes have been in the fire, as well as God's people. Both the promise and the precept are in the furnace, and if I hang up in the smoke like a bottle, I see hanging up by my side God's commands, covered with soot and smoke, subject to the same perils. Suppose I am persecuted. It is a comfort to know that men do not persecute me but my Master's truth. It is a singular thing, with regard to all the envenomed shafts that have been hurled at me, that they have generally fallen on that part of my frame which is most invulnerable, because they have generally fallen on something I have quoted from somebody else or proved from Scripture. They may go on. It is sweet to think that Jesus Christ is in the smoke as well as we are, and the more flame there is, the better we shall be able to see our Master in the smoke with us.

Another reason why David did not forget the statutes was they were in the soul, where the smoke does not enter. Smoke does not enter the interior of the bottle; it only affects the exterior. So it is with God's children: the smoke does not enter into their hearts. Christ is there, and grace is there, and Christ and grace are both unaffected by the smoke. Come up, clouds of smoke! Curl upward till you envelop me! Still will I hang on the Nail, Christ Jesus—the sure Nail, which never can be moved from its place—and I will feel that "even though our outward man is perishing, yet the inward man is being renewed day by day." And the statutes being there, I do not forget them. "For I am become like a bottle in the smoke; yet do I not forget thy statutes."

To such of you as can join with David, let me give a word of consolation. If you have been persecuted and still hold fast by God's Word, if you have been afflicted and still persevere in the knowledge of our Lord and Master, you have every reason to believe yourself a Christian. If under your trials and troubles you remain just what you were when at ease, you may then hope, and not only so, but steadfastly believe and be assured that you are a child of God.

I know—poor, weak, and helpless though I am—that I have a rich Almighty Friend. If you can stand a little smoke, then you may believe yourself to be a child of God. But there are some fantastic people we know of who are shocked with a very puff of smoke. They cannot endure it—they go out at once, just like rats out of the hold of a ship when they begin to smoke it. But if you can live in the smoke and say, "I feel it and still can endure it," if you can stand a smoky sermon and endure a smoky trial and hold fast to God under a smoky persecution, then you have reason to believe that you are certainly a child of God.

Fair-weather birds! You are good for nothing; it is the stormy petrels that are God's favorites. He loves the birds that can swim in the tempest; He loves those who can move in the storm and, like the eagle, can make the wind their chariot, and ride upon forked flames of fire. If in the heat of battle, when your helmet is bruised by some powerful enemy, you can still hold up your head, and say, "I know whom I have believed," and do not swerve from your post, then you are verily a child of heaven. For constancy, endurance, and perseverance are the true marks of a hero of the cross and of the invincible warriors of the Lord.

Those are no invincible ships that flee away before a storm. He is no brave warrior who hears reports from others that a fort is impregnable and dares not attack it. But he is brave who dashes his ship beneath the guns or runs her well-nigh aground and gives broadside after broadside with a desperate valor against his foe. He who in the smoke and the tempest, in the clamor and roar of the battle, can yet coolly give his commands and, knowing that every man is expected to do his duty, can fight valiantly—he is a brave commander, he is a true soldier, he shall receive from his Master a crown of glory. O Christian! Cleave to your Master in the smoke, hold on to your Lord in the trials, and you shall be refined by your afflictions.

However, I have some here who can consume their own smoke. There are some of my congregation who, when they have any trials, can manage to get over them very well themselves. They say, "Well, I don't care, you seem to be a sad set of simpletons. You feel everything; but as for me, it all rolls off, and I don't care for anything." No, I dare say, you do not. But the time will come when you will find the truth of that little story you used to read when you were children, that those who don't care came to a very bad end. These persons are not like bottles in the smoke but like pieces of wood hanging over it. They will soon find there is something more than smoke. They will come to a place where there is not only smoke but fire. And though they can endure the smoke of this world's troubles, they will find it not so easy as they imagine to endure the unutterable burnings and the everlasting flames of that pit whose fire knows no extinction and whose worm shall know no death.

Oh! hardened sinner, you have sorrows now, which are like the skirmishers before an army, a few light-armed troops to lead the way for the whole hosts of God's avengers, who shall trample you beneath their feet. One or two drops of woe have fallen on the pavement of your life; you laugh at them. But they are the heralds of a shower of fire and brimstone, which God shall rain out of heaven upon your soul throughout eternity. And yet you may be pitying us poor Christians because of our troubles and sufferings. Pity us, do you? Ah, but our light affliction is but for a moment, and it works for us a far more exceeding and eternal weight of glory. Take your pity back, and reserve it for yourselves, for your light joy, which is but for a moment, works out for you a far more exceeding and eternal weight of torment. Your little bliss will be the mother of an everlasting, unutterable torture, which we shall happily escape. Your sun will soon set, and at its setting your night shall come. And when your night comes, it will be night forever, without hope of light again.

Before your sun sets, my hearer, may God give you grace. Do you inquire what you should do to be saved? Again comes the old answer: "Believe on the Lord Jesus Christ, and you will be saved." If you are no sinner, I have no salvation for you. If you are a Pharisee and do not know your sins, I have no Christ to preach to you; I have no heaven to offer you. But if you are a sinner, a bona fide sinner, if you are a real sinner, not a sham one, I have this to tell you: Jesus Christ came to save sinners, even the chief. And if you will believe on Him, you shall go out of this house of prayer, shriven, absolved, without a sin; forgiven, pardoned, washed, without a stain; accepted in the Beloved. As long as you live that pardon shall avail you; and when you die, you will have nothing to do but to show it at the gates of paradise to gain admittance. And then, in a nobler and sweeter song, that pardon shall form the basis of your praise while heaven's choirs shall sing, or while the praise of the Eternal shall be the chant of the universe. God bless you! Amen.

Acknowledgments

AS WITH ANY WRITING PROJECT, this book would not have come to completion without the sacrifice and support of many. I remain profoundly indebted to each one of them.

At the personal level, my life and ministry are enabled and enriched by the prayers and encouragement of my family. God has given me a wife, Karen, and children, Anne-Marie, Caroline, William, Alden, and Elizabeth, who bless me beyond measure. I love each one of you unconditionally, infinitely more than you'll ever know.

At the institutional level, my colleagues and office staff are an invaluable source of support and encouragement. Most especially, I'm thankful for Tyler Sykora, Dawn Philbrick, Lauren Hanssen, and Justin Love. I'm also thankful for Russ Meek, who provided keen editorial assistance. Each one of these men and women is an absolute delight to serve with, and they each go about their daily tasks with graciousness and competence. Thank you.

I'm thankful to the team at Moody Publishers, most especially Drew Dyck and Allan Sholes. Thank you for believing in this project and for working with me to bring it to completion.

Last, and most of all, I'm indebted to my Lord and Savior, Jesus Christ. Like every other ministerial undertaking, none of this would be possible without His grace, calling, and enabling. May this book, and all that I do, bring Him much glory.

When Spurgeon speaks, you'd be wise to listen.

Volume 1 of the Spurgeon Speaks series collects Spurgeon's reflections on prayer. Known as a mighty man of prayer, his insights will deepen your prayer life too. Presented in lovely editions that you'll be proud to own, the series offers readings on topics of importance to the Prince of Preachers.

978-0-8024-2628-4

Volume 2 of the Spurgeon Speaks series focuses on the power of God's Word. Spurgeon's love for the Bible will encourage you too.

978-0-8024-2629-1

Volume 3 of the Spurgeon Speaks series shows you how to stay strong when life is coming at you hard. Spurgeon himself faced trials—physical challenges, harsh criticism, and much more—yet he stayed focused on God's call for his life. This book will help you do the same.

978-0-8024-2630-7

Volume 4 of the Spurgeon Speaks series helps you find true rest—the lasting peace that comes from confidence in God. Spurgeon points you to the biblical promises God has made. Those words weren't just valid for ancient Israelites or Victorian-era preachers. God's eternal promises can give you rest today!

978-0-8024-2631-4

also available as eBooks

MOODY
Publishers®

From the Word **to Life**®

AS A PASTOR,
DO YOU FEEL LIKE YOU'RE
WEARING TOO MANY HATS?

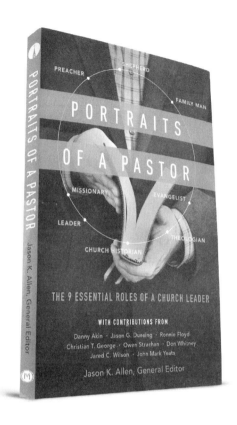

MOODY
Publishers®

*From the Word **to** Life®*

Portraits of a Pastor features contributions from leading evangelical pastors on the essential roles and aspects of pastoral ministry. Together the book answers three important questions: What does it mean for the pastor to hold all nine roles? *Why* should the pastor fulfill these roles? How can the pastor most faithfully fulfill them?

978-0-8024-1634-6 | also available as an eBook

Collected insights from A.W. Tozer on common topics for the Christian life

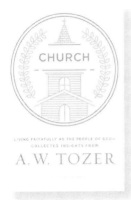

978-0-8024-1828-9

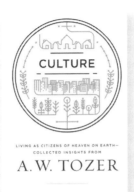

978-1-60066-801-2

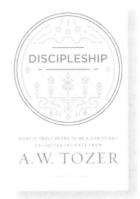

978-1-60066-804-3

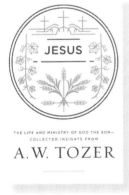

978-0-8024-1520-2

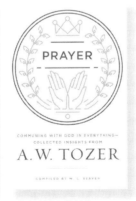

978-0-8024-1381-9

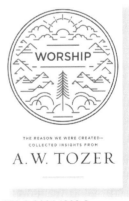

978-0-8024-1603-2

also available as eBooks

BRINGING YOU *timeless classics*

Selected for their enduring excellence and timeless perspective, these are key books that every believer on the journey of spiritual formation should read.

MOODY
Publishers®

From the Word to Life®